MW00682938

Published by To His Glory Publishing Company, Inc.®

111 Sunnydale Court

Lawerenceville, GA 30044 U.S.A.

www.tohisglorypublishing.com

Testimonial

"Wherefore, my dearly beloved, flee from idolatry"
1 Corinthians 10:14 (KJV)

"Since the days of the early church, Christians have held to many pagan ideas while professing to live a Bible-centered life. Ms. Ogenaarekhua does a good job of exposing the works of the enemy while providing hope for all believers—young and old. This book is guaranteed to activate the body of Christ into a deeper hunger for Truth and Revelation of the Word.

"Mary Ogenaarekhua was raised from the dead to deliver truth to the body of Christ. Let he who has an ear hear what the Spirit of God is speaking this day."

—*Rev. Suzanne M. Rogers*

"This is a very eloquent story of God shedding His light in our dark places, and of His plan and purpose unfolding and manifesting in our lives regardless of where we've been. I believe that this book has the Lord's anointing all over it, and that many lives will be touched by it."

—*Lisa Nkala*

"I thank God for the privilege of knowing Mary. The Lord has placed on the inside of her some of the most wonderful and powerful gifts of the Holy Spirit. *Unveiling the God-Mother*, as revealing as it is, is only a small glimpse into the wellspring of Mary's God-given anointings. I believe that this work is ordained by God and for all those led to read it, their lives and their understanding of Christian celebrations will be forever changed, launching the body of Christ into a more powerful sainthood and further preparation for the end times."

—Rhonda W. Cook

Deuteronomy 7:16, 26

16. Do not look on them with pity and do not serve their gods, for that will be a snare to you.
26. Do not bring a detestable thing into your house or you, like it, will be set apart for destruction. Utterly abhor and detest it, for it is set apart for destruction.

"As God instructed the children of Israel to destroy those who live in the land HE promised to give to them, He warned them not to serve idol gods. The Ten Commandments states, "Thou shalt have no other gods before me." We must remember that GOD is the same GOD now as when He brought the children of Israel out of Egypt. HE cannot, HE will not, and HE has not changed. THIS BOOK WILL INDEED OPEN YOUR EYES TO SPIRITUAL TRUTH AS IT RELATES TO THE CHURCH IN THE NOW."

—Irish M. Wimbush

Unveiling the God-Mother

Mary J. Ogenaarekhua

Unveiling the God-Mother

Scriptures are quoted from the Dake's Annotated Reference Bible (King James Version).

"Semiramis and Tammuz," "Indrani and Child," and "Diana of Ephesus" illustrations on p. 73 originally appeared in *The Two Babylons*. "Isis and Horus" and "Devaki and Crishna" illustrations on p. 73 originally appeared in *Die Romische Kirche-Mysterien-Religion aus Babylon* (German edition). Sketch on p. 74 by Hananiah Harrison. Illustration on p. 88 by Otto Von. Illustration on p. 109 reproduced by permission of Chick Publications.

International Standard Book Number: 1-58736-280-5
Library of Congress Control Number: 2003115512

Dedication

To my Lord and Savior, who paid the ultimate price for me to have a second chance in life. Lord, for all that you have done for me and have seen me through, I thank you. May this book be to the praise and glory of your name. Be magnified by this book.

To Deaconess Patricia Gbadamosi, my mother. Thank you for being my mother. Your ministry continues to inspire me. I love you and I thank you for showing me how to live the true Christian life. You are truly an example of those who talk the talk and walk the walk.

To my brothers, Gabriel and Ayo, and my sisters, Josephine, Philomena, and Bridget. God has used each one of you at some point in my life as a chisel to mold and shape me in my journey through life. I love you all.

To John Sado, my elementary school teacher, who sometimes paid for my schoolbooks with his own money. You were determined to make sure that my brother and I got an education. Thank you for your sacrifice.

To my little twelve-year-old hero (an Ibo boy) whose name I can no longer remember but who gave me the equivalent of $20 that he won in a pool game to pay my first term tuition in high school. You took me to your high school and demanded that your teacher place me in class, because by your assessment I was too intelligent to just learn typing. You were an angel in my path. God bless you.

To Bennett Izeh, who was there for me in my teenage years.

To all who hate idolatry and desire spiritual truth.

To all those who desire to worship only the one True God.

Contents

Preface

Most of us see ourselves as simply living from one day to another without really understanding the impact that we have on other people, and the impact that other people have on us as we journey through life. We do not understand what an extraordinary life (good or bad) we have lived until we come into the Kingdom of God and the Lord begins to help us review our lives in order to see where we have been and why. He does this to help us who believe in Him to understand His plan and purpose for our lives. The Bible says in Proverbs 29:18 that **"Where there is no vision (purpose), the people perish."** You will discover from reading this book that God will use every experience in our lives to help us understand the purpose He has for us. I wondered over the years about the things that I have been through, without success, until I received the Lord as my Savior. As the Lord helped me to review my life, I began to see that there was a common thread in my experiences that I thought were just life's way of dealing me a bad hand. You will see from reading about my experiences that God places you in the family, places, and nation that will give you the opportunities (not all good) that will create hunger and thirst for your purpose in life. Only when you receive the Lord Jesus as your personal Lord and Savior can you begin to understand your true purpose in life. Here you will read the story of an African child growing up in Africa and what happened when the Lord Jesus came into her life.

Acknowledgments

Rhonda Cook, I am truly grateful for your help and inspiration throughout the duration of this project. You are a true friend, yes, a real Jonathan to me. Thank God for using you to help me get to work on...The book! The book! The book! T.C. (Tim): see, I did not forget you. God used you to bring Rhonda and me together. Thanks for your interest in this project and for your sense of humor.

Suzanne Rogers, you are a true sister in the Lord. Thank you for your input that resulted in the reorganization of this work. You encouraged me.

I take my hat off for David and Joyce Smith. Thank you for interviewing me on your TV program (Channel 57). It gave me a lot of exposure.

Irish Wimbush and Regina Kinnie, you two are awesome. Thank you both for being there for me during the most critical stage of this project. I could not have done it without your help. Irish, thank you for editing the second-draft copy.

Lisa Nkala, thank you a million times for your support, encouragement, and the dream. It came to pass as you saw it. I give glory to God.

Pastor Chris Oyakhilome, thanks for your faithfulness in the service of the Lord. On October 28, 1992, you advised me to turn the steering wheel of my life over to the Lord. When you led me in the sinner's prayer that day in your office little did I know of what the Lord had in store for me. Yes, God is His Word!

Bishop Theo Ogbah, thanks for your courage in confronting me with the truth concerning Semiramis and for your encouragement after reading part of this work.

Rhonda Hammerstrom, thanks for editing the first draft of this work. Keep the faith.

Hananiah Harrison, I think you did a great job with the artwork on the "Madonna." It took a little fixing but it worked! Thank you.

Obasi Scott, thank you for your work on the cover of this book. You are a true pro!

Chapter One

✌✌

The Author's Background

I grew up in Jattu, a small Muslim town in Edo State, Nigeria. My dad renounced Islam and accepted Christianity when he was a little boy. Therefore, when I was born, he named me Justina. In 1994 the Lord gave me the name Mary, so now I go by Mary Justina. According to my grandmother, I took my first baby steps before the age of one but I suddenly stopped walking not long after. Nobody could explain why I stopped walking. After seeking help from the hospital in a nearby town and after several visits to several witch doctors, nothing seemed to help restore my limbs. After about two years, when everyone had given up hope of my ever walking again, I suddenly began to walk when no one was looking!

The people in Jattu had earlier rejected the missionaries and Christianity and had chosen Islam as the official religion of the town. The practice of Christianity was not permitted. Therefore, in my early years, I heard no teaching on the Lord Jesus Christ in the house where I grew up.

In Jattu, there was a great thirst for supernatural powers. Most people had a vast knowledge of the supernatural in relation to witchcraft activities and strange spiritual occurrences. Getting hold of supernatural power for protection was a driving force in the life of many. They needed protection from

witches, from evil spirits that suddenly appear in people's homes, from their enemies, from sickness and
diseases. Most of the people adhered to Islam but a
great number kept their pagan practices like consult-
ing witch doctors and divination, and they practiced
them alongside Islam.

My family in particular also believed in the god of
iron (*Ogun* or *Umomi*). It is the god that my ancestors
worshipped before Islam came along. My grandfather
was a retired blacksmith, and one of my uncles took
over the business and worked at the shop during the
day, but because the shop was also the shrine for
Ogun or Umoni, at night or in the evening, my uncle
would use the shop as the place of sacrifice to the idol
while we watched. This god demands blood sacri-
fices and wine poured out as libation (i.e., pouring
wine on the ground, iron, or stone) in its worship. We
worshipped this idol accordingly as well as observed
other religious practices alongside Islam. The towns-
people feared the god Umomi because it is believed
that he is the god of vengeance. The belief is that he
does not forgive anyone who is guilty of an offence
and refuses to confess the guilt. Therefore, the service
of this god was frequently demanded. Whenever the
guilty party needed to be exposed in a dispute, we little children in the house were sometimes called upon
to go and execute the vengeance of Umomi. We would
go to the house where there was a dispute and pro-
nounce curses on the guilty party for six nights. The
belief is that the guilty party will swell up and die
within three months if the person does not confess
the guilt before the seventh night.

Therefore, growing up with my grandmother and
the pagan practices in our house, I learned about idol
worship, Islam, consultation with witch doctors, and

divination. I also witnessed the thirst of the towns-people for acquisition of supernatural power. As a child, I accompanied my grandmother on a weekly basis to her personal witch doctor. Although she was officially a Muslim, my grandmother was more inter-ested in the supernatural via divination and witch doctors than the practice of Islam. She frequently boasted of how her father had a reputation of being the most powerful witch doctor in his day. She grew up in the midst of supernatural powers of the dark side. She loved me and my brother and all the other grandchildren that she cared for. Therefore, she sought to protect us the best way she could.

One day a "medicine man" (one who claims to have supernatural power but does not regard himself as a witch doctor) came to the local weekly open mar-ket in Jattu. He was looking for those who needed protection from snake and scorpion bites. My grand-mother knew that I sometimes went with the older children to the woods to hunt for crickets and locusts. I loved to eat them. She wanted to protect my brother and me from snakes and scorpions, so she told us to go over to the man to receive the protection. She paid him and he made several marks on the back of our palms and on our feet and rubbed the "medi-cine" he had brought with him on them. He wanted to demonstrate the unfailing protection and power that he had given to us, so he took off the hat on his head and a scorpion fell out. He instructed my broth-er to pick it up and he did. Afterwards he requested that I pick it up and I did. He also had a snake, but I drew the line with the snake, but my brother picked it up. We went home feeling very protected from scorpi-ons and snakes.

Not long afterwards, it was very hot one night and as we usually did when it was too hot, we took our mats outside to sleep in the open air. While I was asleep, someone heard me gasping for breath in my sleep and woke up. When I was turned over on my mat, they discovered that my arm had turned black, which is an indication that a scorpion had stung me while I was asleep. They lifted my pillow from the mat and, sure enough, the scorpion had crawled under my pillow! The day before, another "medicine man" had come to the shop of one of my uncles. This uncle had in his youth lost one of his legs due to snakebite. The man sold him a little potion of black liquid (*gbog-boeshe*). The man said the potion was an antidote for scorpion and snakebites. My uncle immediately brought out the black potion, mixed it with water and gave it to me to drink. Also by God's divine intervention, my grandmother took the necessary steps to quickly get me to the town's pharmacist who promptly gave me an injection! It saved my arm.

Over the years, I sometimes wondered why I was the only one who got stung out of the group of us that slept outside that night. The Lord knew this, so years later, after I got born again, the Lord said to me concerning the scorpion incident, "I had to show your grandmother the extent of the so-called protection she thought she had purchased for you."

Again a man appeared in the town and claimed to have supernatural power to lift heavy things off the ground. His name was "Killiwee." The townspeople came out en masse to watch as he lifted cars and heavy objects off the ground. Somehow he faded away.

Afterwards another man came from one of the neighboring towns. He boasted of all kinds of

supernatural powers from India. He claimed to consult with different types of spirits as well as possess
the ability to charm snakes. We heard that during one
of his demonstrations, one of his snakes fatally bit
him. The report that flooded the town was that
before he died, he told the people in his hometown
not to worry because he would "rise again" on the
third day. Most people who had been to his shows in
Jattu, including myself, counted the days to the
supernatural "resurrection" on the third day. The
third day came and went and he never rose from the
dead. We were all disappointed.

Not long after came another witch doctor boasting of great powers. His claim was that he had the
ability to anoint a person with power so that no
object whatsoever (bullets or knives) would penetrate
the person's body. To prove his point, he requested a
volunteer from his audience. My Uncle Amedu's first
son, Patrick, was very grown at this time. He wanted
Patrick to receive this great power, and so he instructed Patrick to go and be the first person to receive this
great power. Men, women, and us little children gathered together to observe this awesome demonstration
of supernatural power. He asked for a well-sharpened
machete (cutlass) and it was brought to him. He told
Patrick to take off his shirt and then proceeded to
anoint Patrick's back and shoulders with his "medicine." When he was done, he instructed Patrick that
he was going to pursue Patrick with the machete, but
that Patrick should not run too fast because he needed to use the machete on Patrick's back. He assured
Patrick that nothing bad would happen to him. He
told Patrick that he had given several people this
power before and that Patrick would be amazed at the
demonstration of this supernatural power on him.

We watched in awe as he pursued Patrick and as he raised the machete and cut Patrick on the shoulder! There was blood all over Patrick's shoulder and back! The man kept on running and never stopped to look back at the mob running after him to lynch him. Thus, he ran for his life with the multitude of us who were at the scene pursuing him. We never caught up with him. It is quite amazing how fast a man can run when he knows that his very life depends on it!

On another occasion, one of my aunts became sick and she was taken to a well-reputed witch doctor in another town for treatments. My grandmother suggested that I go with her so that I could help her run errands in the town. We went for about a week. The man had people with various forms of mental illness locked up in different rooms of his house as patients. Because this man also had a reputation of being able to call up the souls of the newly departed (i.e., people who have just died), the majority of his clients were people who had just lost loved ones in neighboring towns and wanted the opportunity to say goodbye. In my curiosity, I sneaked around his house for evidence of newly departed souls and I found none. But it was obvious that the house was full of eerie darkness. After one week of his so-called power, my aunt was not any better, so we went back home.

I became so disappointed because none of the men who boasted of great supernatural powers could back them up. I was particularly disappointed in the power of my grandmother's personal witch doctor. Before we made our weekly visit to him, she would sometimes talk about how great or powerful a witch doctor the man was and I would wonder about the statement because I never saw a demonstration of the man's spiritual power.

Then one day when I was about the age of seven or eight years old, the Lord Jesus decided to come and introduce Himself to me and to show me TRUE SUPERNATURAL POWER. I had what I thought was a dream (the Lord told me after I got saved that it was an actual visitation and not a dream). *In this dream, I was outside of the house in the open air in the middle of the night. I looked up and I saw from a distance something that looked like the silhouette of a man descending from the blue sky. I wanted to get a closer look at the figure so I began to follow it. I found myself on this narrow path of nothing but green trees and the clear blue sky. I began to run after the figure. The more I ran after this figure the more it moved just ahead of me, but it was getting more and more visible and larger in size. Finally I arrived on the top of a mountain and the man clothed only in a white loincloth descended from the sky and landed on the top of the mountain. When His feet touched the mountain, the mountain divided into two and the bottom of it became a huge valley filled with red-hot coals! Because I was so little I lay flat on my stomach to get a better view of the bottom of the valley without falling into it. When I did this, I saw Him walking barefoot on the red-hot coals, and His feet were not burnt! The red-hot coals did not bother him. His SUPERNATURAL POWER mesmerized me!! Here it was at last, the supernatural power. A thought occurred to me: "How is He going to get out from the bottom of this enormous deep valley?" I immediately cried out to Him, "I cannot carry you up by myself because I am too little," and He with a very broad smile looked up at me and replied in English, "Don't worry; I'll be right up." Before He finished the sentence, He was standing right beside me on top of the mountain! I was shocked at how he could perform such* *a supernatural feat. He just simply asked me, "Everyone is sleeping, why are you not asleep?" and I replied, "I was asleep but then I saw you." He stretched out His right hand and laid it on my forehead and said with a smile, **"Go and get yourself baptized and I will show you many things."*** That was the end of the dream.

Although He did not tell me His name, I knew Him as my friend in the dream that could walk on red-hot coals without His feet getting burnt. His strength could make a mountain split in two and become a valley when He stood on it. He was my friend who could actually demonstrate supernatural power without boasting. The Lord, being "all knowing," was aware that I had not yet heard about Him or about Christianity. He chose to introduce Himself to me in this visitation as the one who has all power and can truly do the impossible. I saw the power that most people I knew in Jattu were yearning to see. Because I did not know about Christianity or His name, I kept the dream to myself.

After the visitation, I began to challenge the so-called abilities of the witch doctors and "medicine" men. Something strange began to happen to me also. When my grandmother and I would make our visits to the witch doctor's house, and as soon as my grandmother would make her request to him about the things she wanted him to consult the underworld spirits for, I would give her some of the answers before the witch doctor had a chance to open his mouth to do his divination. She informed my grandfather about my sudden ability to see things in the spirit. They made a decision that I was not to tell anyone about it. Personally, I did not want to explore what was happening to me because most of the things I saw made me afraid. Furthermore, I saw them infrequently and I had no idea what most of them meant. Because I was so young, I did not know at the time that it was as a result of the Lord's visitation. He had laid His hands on my forehead before He left.

On another visitation to the witch doctor by my grandmother (without me, because I did not like going with her anymore), he informed my grandmother that a plague would come upon my entire family if the god Umomi or Ogun that was housed in my family was not appeased. According to him, the god had favored my family. Therefore, he (the god) sent his mother to my family as a sign of this special favor upon my family, but my family had disrespected him by not acknowledging his mother. As a result, the god was angry and was getting ready to plague my family for the disrespect. She came home and again informed my grandfather. She got my grandfather's permission to go ahead and make the necessary preparations to appease the god.

She announced that the witch doctor identified me as the "god-mother" of my family idol god Ogun. Therefore, on an appointed day, yours truly was officially installed as the "god-mother" with the title "Ogun!" During the ceremony, all I cared about was the privilege that I was now given to choose whatever part of the chicken I wanted before everyone else who qualifies to eat the sacrifice to this idol. The rule was that for every sacrifice offered to this god, (which was usually a live chicken or goat); I had to pour the blood on my grandfather's huge blacksmith stone, which was also used as the shrine of this idol. What I thought was the best part of the deal about being "god-mother" was the announcement that from the day of the ceremony on, no member of my family or anyone else was permitted to hit or touch my head without incurring the anger of this very revengeful god. **Everyone was to reverence my head.** I quickly discovered that the other children did not like the idea of playing with some god or god-mother as the title suggested. Therefore, I hated the title Ogun because it made the other children afraid of me, so I refused to answer to it. As a result, the name did not stick.

Some months after the Lord's visitation in which He laid His Hand on my head, and after the ceremony to install me as "god-mother," the Lord demonstrated His supernatural power in my life. **He raised me up from the dead.** About three days before this particular day, I was out playing in the rain with some children when we came across a newly dug grave for a non- Muslim elderly woman who had died. When I looked into the grave, I saw all the earthworms that were crawling in it because of the rain. I remember declaring to the other children that I would never go into a grave. I did not know how quickly that statement would come to pass. A couple of days later, I took a fatal fall from the staircase in a neighbor's house around 8 or 9 p.m. while playing with some of my friends. That neighbor had gone to bed early and her husband was away for the weekend in the city. One of her daughters and her stepdaughter were among the friends I was playing with in her house.

We were playing with a very long pole that had to be lifted above the heads of about four carriers on both ends while we each took turns sitting in the middle, enjoying the ride. I had seen a Chinese gymnastics magazine not too long before this time and I wanted to try what I saw in the magazine. Therefore, when it was my turn to sit on the pole, I decided to put into practice what I had seen in the Chinese magazine. I requested that we climb up the staircase to the top of the stairs since there was light in the hallway. Everything was great and I had the thrill I wanted as they raised the pole above their heads and I was sitting on it while we went up the stairs. When we got to the top of the stairs, I decided to stand on the pole just like in the magazine while the pole was still raised and give a victory shout. As I began the process of trying to stand on the pole from a sitting position so that I could give a triumphant shout of victory, I did not know that there was still one last stair step left to climb. Those at the bottom end of the pole were taking their last step up the stairs as I was getting up to stand on the pole. As they stepped up to the last stair and before I could utter a word, I fell headfirst onto the metal bannister of the stairs and bounced headlong onto the stairs. I then tumbled all the way to the bottom of the stairs! Before the body tumbled to the last step at the bottom of the stairs, I was already separated from my body and was above them and I began to watch them as they became shocked and horrified at what had happened. Even they could not immediately utter a word because it happened so fast. They then tried unsuccessfully to get a response from the body without waking up my friend's mother. Because they knew that they would get into serious trouble, they made a pact not to tell anyone what had happened. Because I felt fine where I was and I was not in any pain, their actions did not bother me. I saw each one of them sneak back into their homes and go to sleep. About 6:30 a.m. or so, my friend's mother woke up, and she discovered the body at the bottom of her stairs. Her screams woke up those around her, including the people in our house across the street. I watched them as they cried and as they wanted to know what had happened. They said that because of the hours involved before the body was discovered, it was already cold and stiff (rigor mortis).

They decided to make funeral arrangements to have the body buried at noon. A message was sent to the local king's palace because my grandparents were officially Muslims. They were given a plot in the town's Muslim cemetery. They dug the grave and prepared the body (i.e., washed and wrapped the body tight in white cloth) for burial. I watched all the commotion that was going on. I knew as soon as I was separated from my body that I was in a different dimension from them. I did not even try to speak to anyone because I was aware that they could not hear me. I also knew that they did not know that I was around watching everything they were doing. All I could do was watch them as you watch a television. At about noon, I saw one of the two men who were to head the little procession to the Muslim cemetery pick up the body. The one had the Koran while the other carried the body in his arms because the Muslims do not bury in a casket. There was a carriage in the town's mosque that was used to carry the dead bodies of Muslim adults to the cemetery and was returned back to the mosque, but a dead child's body was just picked up and taken to the cemetery.

Before starting out for the cemetery, the man who had the Koran wanted to know what name he was to use in prayer as they headed out to the cemetery. Therefore he asked, "What is the child's name?" Someone answered "Justina." In an instant, the man who carried the body dropped it like a hot potato! Both he and the man that had the Koran were furious at my grandfather for calling them to bury a Christian! They left the body on the floor and went

away in anger and I just watched. Because my grandfather was a chief at the king's palace, he decided to
use his position of influence with the Muslim king to
get the body accepted into the cemetery, but the
answer was "no" from the king and the other chiefs.
They said that on no account would a Christian be
accepted into the cemetery. He argued unsuccessfully
in his attempt to convince them that he and my
grandmother were my legal guardians. My dad had
remained missing years after the end of the
Nigerian/Biafra war, so my grandparents were my
guardians. The answer was still no. The counterargu-
ment was that my dad had renounced Islam and
become a Christian and so by their summation, I was
a Christian!

My parents were divorced before I was four years
old, and my mother had remarried and was living in
another state (Lagos) with her husband. Both my
grandparents with whom I grew up knew nothing
about Christianity. My grandfather never really forgave my dad for his decision to become a Christian
and he was particularly angry with my dad on this day
for giving me the name "Justina." It now created a
dilemma for him concerning the funeral. Since my
dad was not around to make any decision, one of my
dad's older sisters announced that she could go to the
neighboring town where they have a church and call
the priest to come and take the body away for a
Christian funeral. I watched them as my grandmother interrupted her by reminding her that my mother
had actually wanted to take me with her when she was
leaving my dad and that it was this aunt who
snatched me away from my mother's arms. She told
her that if it was a Muslim funeral that was
conducted as planned, my mother would understand

because she knew that the Muslim custom was to bury a body the same day, but if it was going to be a Christian funeral as it seemed, they at least owed my mother the opportunity to say goodbye to her child.

Prior to this day, I had thought that my grandparents were my actual parents. It was a surprise for me to learn as I listened to their conversations that I had another mother. I was very curious to know who she was and what she looked like. They decided to keep the body in a room while someone went to Lagos to inform my mother of what had happened. They gave a man, a relative, the transportation fare to go to Lagos and get my mother. I was very interested in this man's errand so I followed him to the motor park in the next town and I watched as they finally got enough passengers to fill the taxi before heading off to Lagos on a three- to four-hour journey. I followed the taxi to Lagos and watched as the man broke the news to my mother.

Now, I had seen the reactions of the different ones in the village as they heard the news of what had happened to me. I had watched their crying, but I had never seen a grown-up person cry as much as I saw this woman whom they said was my mother cry. Most of the people cried when they heard the news, but after a while they stopped; but not this woman. She was devastated. Her crying grew more and more intense by the hour. I watched her as she hurriedly got a few things together and set out with the messenger back to the motor park in Lagos for a taxi that would bring them back to Jattu. When the taxi finally had enough passengers, they headed out on the journey back. Halfway back to the village, I was moved with so much compassion for this woman that the only thing I thought about was making it back to the room where the body was kept before she did. I had to get back into my body so that when she stepped into the room, she would see that I was all right. **I just wanted her to stop crying.**

When you are separated from your body, your desire becomes your means of transportation or vehicle. I knew that I could outrun the taxi that she was in and make it to the room before her. I did; praise God! When she stepped into the room at about 9 or 10 p.m., I got up and sat down, and everyone else fled from the room except her!

Because I was so young, I could not connect my encounter with my Almighty friend (the Lord Jesus) in the dream a few months earlier with my coming back to life from the dead. I did not know the significance of His right hand on my forehead and the blessing it represented. I thought that I just got lucky to come back alive after having been dead. It was after I got saved that He explained to me that because my dad had renounced Islam and became a Christian, therefore He (the Lord Jesus) had the obligation to honor the covenant that my dad made with Him at my birth. He is a God that keeps covenant. He said that although as a little child I was running around with lots of Muslim children, yet there was a spiritual difference between them and me because of the covenant my dad made with Him on my behalf. Also, according to Him, while the events concerning my death were going on in Nigeria, there was a certain Saint in the United States of America (Kathryn Kuhlman) who in her payer time saw a vision of the Muslims as they were rejecting my body. He said that Kathryn prayed to the Lord on my behalf. According to the Lord, she said, "Lord, I guess you will have to raise her up and use her for your glory." The Lord answered her prayer. He also made me understand that it was the very place He blessed (my forehead) that first landed on the metal rail handle of the stairs before my body tumbled down the concrete cement stairs. He also informed me that the visitation that I thought was a dream a few months before the fall was actually my encounter with Him when my spirit was separated from my body. He then explained to me that events usually happen in the spirit realm long before they are manifested in the physical earth. He used Himself as an example. As the Lamb of God, He was slain from before the foundation of the world in the spirit realm, but it took thousands of years before it was manifested on earth! He further explained to me that because I had not heard the Gospel before my fall, He had to come to me as "the Resurrection and the Life" to preach the Gospel to me and to deliver me from the devil's plans against my soul. He simply concluded his explanation to me saying, "you needed the Resurrection and the Life and I was there for you."

When life was back to normal for me, my mother decided to come to Jattu to steal my brother and me from the school we were attending so that we could be with her instead of my grandparents. Unfortunately for her, I had just been told by the wife of one of my uncles during a fight with one of her children that when my mother found out that she was pregnant with me, she wanted to have an abortion because she thought she was pregnant with me too soon after the birth of my brother. She told me in a very hurtful way that if my dad had not held a knife to my mother's throat as a threat of what he would do to her if she successfully aborted me, that I would not have been born. She told me that I did not have any business beating up her children who were very wanted/desired children by her. From that day I became angry with my mother and I began to resent her even though she was not around. Whatever love and emotional feeling I had for her after the fall quickly disappeared. I transferred my affection to my dad and I longed for the day that he would be found alive. Therefore, when my mother brought a car to my elementary school to secretly steal my brother and me away, I refused to get in the car or go anywhere with her. She was very hurt at my reaction to her but I could not tell her why I wanted nothing to do with her. She stared at me for what seemed like eternity with tears in her eyes and she became angry for what she thought was my grandparents brainwashing me against her. She told me that if I did not want to go with her that she would just take my brother. I said, "fine," and she left with my brother. This was the day that I first knew that my brother truly loves me. Not long into the journey with my mother, he had a change of mind. He told my mother that if I did not go, he too would not. Moreover, he told her that I would get killed at the boys and girls elementary school we were both attending if he was not around to protect me. Because I knew that my brother had the reputation of being the strongest student in the school, I felt free to pick on students who got bad grades. Therefore, someone (usually a boy) would beat me up any day my brother did not come to school or any day he left school early. He told my mother to bring him back and she did. Because of this incident, I thought that my mother never forgave me for rejecting her that day. Until I got saved in 1992, I could not really forgive her for trying to abort me and I could still remember the expression of hurt on her face before they drove off that day. I never discussed it with her but I nursed a secret grudge against her without her knowledge.

My dad returned alive after surviving being locked up in an underground bunker for an additional three years after the Nigeria/Biafra war ended. He was one of three hundred civilians locked up by the Biafran soldiers, and only he and about ten others survived the ordeal. He had a hero's welcome when he was released. I remember how we were dismissed from my elementary school early on the day of his return so that we could participate in the welcome-home ceremony. I guess because of what he went through during the time of his captivity, he did not turn out to be the dad I had expected. He shattered the childhood image I had built up in my mind concerning him and his return. For instance, about three days after his return, my grandmother decided that my brother and I should start having dinner with him in order to get to know him. Dinner was usually served to him outside in front of the house. On our second or third dinner with him, there was a little incident with my brother. I got two chairs for my dad and me and I wanted my brother to get his own chair. When I went to get water for us all, my brother took my chair. I insisted that he give me back my chair and he refused. My dad got very angry with me and he commanded my brother, saying, "Give her a dirty slap," and when my brother refused, he turned around and gave my brother a slap that shattered my expectations and my affection for him. My grandmother disapproved of adults using unnecessary force against children, so she told my dad off. I was glad because I most certainly did not want to have any further contact with him. I did not want to eat with him or stay around him after that.

Then one day (still within three months of his return), I went to pick mangoes in the forest. I climbed up to a branch that was too high on the tree, so when I began shaking the other branches in order to get the mangoes to fall off, the branch that I was sitting on broke off and I fell off the tree. When I landed on the ground, my right hand got stuck on a tree branch that was already on the ground. Because the splinter was embedded deep into my palm, I could not get it out, so I went home and showed my hand to my dad. I was shocked when he grabbed my hand and just yanked out the splinter without so much as a word of comfort before or afterwards.

On another day, he was distributing money to all the little children who were in our neighborhood, as he normally did whenever he was in town, and I joined the children to receive money also. I watched as he gave money to all the other children and he drove me away saying that I should go to my grandparents. I was horrified by his lack of affection towards me. I was so angry with him that I said some very hurtful words to him.

Despite these and other unpleasant incidents with my dad, my dad was one of the kindest persons that I ever knew when it involved other people. I think that he sincerely believed that my brother and I did not really need him because we had my grandparents and my mother. Therefore, he was there to help anyone that he could possibly help except my brother and me. I greatly resented it. I would watch as he went beyond the call of duty in his attempts to help people. Although he was not rich, he would give whatever he had to needy families, find schools, and pay tuitions for very bright students who had no one to help them financially. God gave him the anointing to have great

influence with people. If you wanted to meet someone prominent and you did not know how to go
about it, you went to my dad and he would either give
you a note (a guarantee that the person would see
you) or he would take you and introduce you to the
person. It was incredible how he seemed to personally know a lot of prominent people. He had a reputation of being one of the most intelligent men of his
days. He was a full-fledged schoolteacher by the age of
sixteen! We heard stories of how the school principal
had to provide him a stool to stand on in order for
him to be able to write on the board because he was so
young and so little. According to my grandmother,
my dad gave up teaching and became a police officer
because some of his students would beat him up
when he gave them bad grades. Some of his students
and children of his former students later became leaders in the country. One day, I ran into him in Benin
City and I followed him into the home of one of the
most prominent leaders in our State. The guards just
gave way out of respect to my dad as we walked right
in. The man was fast asleep at about 2:30 p.m. and my
dad woke him up, saying, "Boy get up, what are you
doing sleeping at midday. I taught you better than
that." All this prominent leader could do was apologize. My dad told him, "I just wanted to check on you
to see how you are doing. I see you are doing fine,"
and we left. Different people would come up to me
and tell me the good things my dad did for them and
their families, and I would get angry because he was
there for everyone else except his own children. I
quickly gave up on him and I just simply regarded my
grandparents as my parents.

   To his credit, he did try for several years to have a
relationship with me, but although I truly loved him,

I was too emotionally wounded by him to desire any relationship with him. He wrote me every chance he got, and I usually responded in anger or just got rid of the letters. I was able to make peace with him in 1993, and in 1994 he died. I learned from my experience with my dad that it is not wise to spend our time on earth in anger against the people God placed in our lives to love. We do not know how much time we have on earth with them. Just when I thought that I could finally have a meaningful relationship with my dad after my salvation, he died.

Not long after my fall, as a little girl, I began to notice that the town's pharmacist and his family would get dressed up on Sundays and go away for some hours, and then they would come back again. The man and his wife were friends with one of my dad's younger sisters. Although I did not know where they normally went to for a few hours, I told my grandmother that I wanted to go with them because my mom had sent me some new clothes and I wanted to wear them. She gave me permission and I went with them. I found out that they went to the Roman Catholic Church in the next town.

After stepping inside the church for the very first time, I looked up and there was an image that looked like my friend from the dream hanging on the wall with the same type of white loincloth on! Because I did not know about graven images yet, I began to scream, "That is my friend from the dream, that's my friend from the dream" to the amazement of those present at the time.

The Lord had told me to go and get baptized, but I did not know what the word "baptism" meant until my last year in elementary school. With the help of my elementary school teachers, I underwent the

Catholic baptism (sprinkling). Apart from the "cate-chisms," I did not learn much from my Sunday church attendance because Mass was celebrated in Latin. I did not know how the Lord wanted me to fol-low Him and the church did not really point me to him. Besides that, I still had to join my grandfather in his Islamic worship. I got discouraged with Islam because I could never complete the one-month fast along with my grandfather. I could not go beyond twelve days or so. You are supposed to make up the days you missed during the rest of the year after Ramadan but I could not make up all the days of fast-ing that I owed. I just simply gave up trying and it left me with a lot of guilt.

When I became aware that there was a book that tells about Jesus, I wanted for years to just hold the book—the Bible—with my hands. I had heard about the Bible but I had never seen one. It was not until my third year in high school that I finally saw a Bible for the very first time. I finally got a Bible because it was a required text in my Bible Literature class. Because I had wanted a Bible for so many years, I could not wait for school to begin before I read it. I immediately took my new Bible and found a quiet place and began to read it. I started from Genesis. I particularly remem-ber Joseph's story because of what his brothers did to him. I found it so touching. I went on to the next book until I got to the place where God commanded Moses and the children of Israel to kill all the Amalekites and not to spare even their women and lit-tle children! I got very angry with the God that would command such a thing. Knowing that most members of my family were Muslims and not Jewish, and that I grew up in a Muslim household, I was exceptionally furious because I could not see where my family and I fit into the God of the Bible's plans. In my anger and rage against the God of the Bible for what I had read in the first two books of the Old Testament, I threw away the Bible! The two things that I remembered in the Old Testament were Joseph's story and Abraham's attempt to sacrifice Isaac. Because I had read the Abraham and Isaac story first in my early years of Islamic study, I thought that the Christians stole it from the Koran. I completed the New Testament religious courses in my third and fourth year in high school. What I learned in the Gospel was just so I could pass my examination. I really did not know what I was supposed to do besides enjoy the stories about Jesus.

I had problems with the religious practice in my boarding school because I did not understand them. For instance, I wanted to know why every evening at 6:00 p.m., a bell would be sounded and every student would come to a standstill no matter what they were doing. I wanted to know what it was all about because it was a strange thing for me to watch. I was told that an angel passed by at the precise time that the bell was sounded. Then I wanted to know why the angel was passing by, what the angel was doing as it passed by, and why I had to stand still to acknowledge it. I did not get a plausible answer so I refused to observe it. The school principal, who was an Irish nun, immediately took note of my protest. What I had read in the Old Testament and the traditions enforced by the nuns at the boarding school actually made me to go back to confessing Islam. I hated the bondage of Islam, so I could not really go the way of Islam again, but as a protest against the God of the Bible, I angrily requested from my high school principal that I should be excused from all the Christian activities

because of Islam. My anger gave me a perfect opportunity to tell the principal that I did not think that I
should be forced to attend the Monday-through-
Friday 6 a.m. Mass. The true reason for my request
was that I hated waking up at 5:30 a.m. to get ready
for Mass. Also, one of my cousins in Lagos had
become a Rosicrucian and I was becoming intrigued
by the mysteries of the Rosicrucian Order (an occult).
My request to be excused from Mass worked for a
whole year. I was the only student on campus who did
not have to wake up at 5:30 a.m. to get ready for Mass!

My perfect excuse was blown one day when my
principal attended an event in some town and she met
someone who knew my dad. She wanted to find out
from the person how to deal with my unwillingness
to participate in the celebration of Mass. The person
(the informant) told her that my dad had actually
renounced Islam and converted to Christianity!
When she came back, she could not wait to let me
know in the most unpleasant way the next morning
at 5 a.m. that she had discovered that my dad was a
Christian. She informed me that since my dad was a
Christian, I was therefore a Christian. She demanded
that from that day on I sit in the front row at every
morning Mass. I resented her duress and I argued that
serving God should be by choice and not by force.
However, before my graduation from high school, I
shared my childhood dream about Jesus with her and
she immediately concluded that the Lord wanted me
to become a nun. She referred me to a priest.

Chapter Two
꩜

Other Spiritual Encounters in My Life

When I was ten years old, I went to live for a while with one of my cousins who had married a Muslim chaplain and moved to the next town. My grandmother wanted me to go and stay with her for a while so that I could run errands for her while she got acclimated to her new environment. Although I was very young, I still remember the man she married as being spiritually diabolical. He was the personal Muslim chaplain for the then president of Nigeria. I remember seeing soldiers and sometimes the president come at night to consult with this man. They were all seeking protection from water spirits. These people would come and tell stories of some strange female "mami-water" (mermaid) spirit that would suddenly manifest itself to them as they conducted their night watches. The president, who was later assassinated, was also seeing the same spirit at his presidential home. I would watch as my cousin's husband wrote verses from the Koran and then wash the writings (ink) into a bowl and give it to them to drink. Every few days the soldiers would come back again because the verses from the Koran that he was giving them to drink did not seem to be effective in driving the spirit away from them. While in this house, I woke up one

morning and found a deep cut with blood on my forehead although I slept alone in my cousin's room that
was locked. My cousin went to spend the night with
her husband in his bedroom and I slept in her room
alone. It was as though someone had dug a large fin-
gernail into my forehead and made a huge cut down
my forehead and then removed the skin on my forehead. I was so scared that I picked up my schoolbooks
and the few clothes I had and I cried all the way home
to show my grandfather what happened. He was not
surprised because he knew about the activities of the
"mamiwater" spirits.

While I was with my cousin, Friday evening
Islamic classes were mandatory for us children in the
house, but the Islamic instructor was one of the most
merciless people that I ever came across in my life.
Along with regular school, we had to memorize the
Koran and be able to recite the portion that we were
assigned without missing a word. The instructor sat
at the back of the class, and the only way he let you
know that you had missed a word or phrase was with
a long whip made of cowhide called "koboko"! This
man would continue to whip a student with his
"koboko" until the student remembered the word or
phrase. Because of this, I dreaded Fridays. To avoid
being a recipient of his merciless whipping, I memo-
rized about half of the Koran in less than six months.
I was so glad when I returned to my grandparents'
home. But I was saddened when the Nigerian president was later assassinated, because I was aware that
he knew that there was a spirit out to kill him and he
so desperately desired to be free of the spirit to no
avail.

When I was in high school, I frequently went to
Lagos for my summer vacation, but because my

mother was married to a man who had three other wives, I preferred to spend most of my time with my cousin Bennett or my uncle in Lagos. My cousin loved children and he would gather us to his apartment and take us to different places designed for kids. At his apartment, we ate all the eggs and bread that we could possibly eat. I mean; I gathered up all the neighborhood children together to eat at his apartment. He was a great cook and he truly enjoyed cooking for us children. When I arrived one summer, I discovered that he had joined a spiritism church (a church called "Aladura" that believed in receiving visions from angels). There are numerous spiritism churches in Nigeria and they do not operate by the Holy Spirit. Their activities are centered on angel worship. The leader of my cousin's church claimed to see visions and therefore could tell people personal things about their lives. One Sunday my cousin took me along to his "newfound" church in Ikoyi and, upon entering the church, the leader pointed to me and shouted, "Stop." He proceeded to tell my cousin and me that he was receiving a vision concerning me. He informed me that I was going to die before I finished high school. I was so upset at his so-called vision that I turned around and told him off before his congregation and walked out. I never went again with my cousin.

On my next visit, I discovered that my cousin had left the first church and had joined another one. This church was also a spiritism church (Aladura). As required of their members, my cousin would dress up on Sundays in a huge white hat, a long flowing white garment, and a yellow sash on his waist, without shoes, and would carry a bell! He would ring the bell all the way to the bus stop in his white robe without any shoes on his way to this church. Because of what happened at the previous church, I said no when he asked me to go with him to this other church. When I went to spend some time with my mother, I discovered that she too had joined an Aladura (spiritism) church and had a long white garment and a huge white hat of her own! Her church allowed them to wear shoes and they did not have to carry a bell. Unlike my cousin Bennett, my mother insisted that I go with her to their all-night prayer. I had no choice in the matter, but because I was not a member, I was not required to wear a long white garment. They had green candles, red candles, and black candles all over the sanctuary. They also had different types of colored water that they give their people to drink. I did not know what it was but I knew that something was not right with their type of worship, so I looked for a corner in the sanctuary and promptly went to sleep. My mother was angry with me on the way home at about six the next morning because I went to sleep in defiance of their leader and her.

When I returned to my cousin's apartment the following summer, I discovered that he had left the Aladura church and that he was now a Rosicrucian. He shared with me some of their beliefs and gave me their magazines to read. I became intrigued with the writings on transcendental meditation, astral projection, and astral travel. Due to my curiosity, I decided to find out what they do, but my cousin was very secretive about their rituals. They were practiced mostly at night. When he thought everyone was asleep, he would step into the kitchen and set up his altar and begin his rituals. I noticed that he did his rituals either on Tuesday or on Thursday nights, so I would allow him time to set up his altar and then secretly watch him. One day he boasted about his Rosicrucian power to put everyone to sleep in the entire neighborhood so that no one could interrupt his activities. What he did not know was that his so-called power could not put me to sleep and that I had observed him almost every time he was conducting his rituals while I was there.

One night, I watched him as he began his transcendental meditation, and as I continued to watch him, I saw him fall on the floor from the chair he was sitting on. I waited a long time and there was no movement from his body. Finally, I went over to the body and began to shake him, but there was no response. It was obvious that he had passed out but he seemed to be breathing fine. As I watched him on the floor and the candles still burning on the altar that he had set up, I thought, how strange that one who claimed to have so much power would pass out in front of his own altar. I did not know if he was on his astral travel or projection so I left the body alone so that his spirit could return into it. As I turned to walk away, I heard a voice like the voice of a baby who is just learning how to talk say to me from the mirror on the altar, "Report, report, report." I went to the altar and I saw my cousin's piece of paper and a pencil on the altar so I concluded that he was probably waiting for the voice to tell him what to write before he passed out. I also saw some images as they began moving through the mirror like a TV, so I decided to see what the images were all about. The voice was telling me to report what I was seeing in the mirror. When I looked closely, I saw that they were images of events that had happened in a photographer's studio before I came to Lagos on my vacation. They were pictures of me and another friend as I tried to show off the new jeans shorts I had recently bought. As far as I was concerned, the pictures or scenes would not be of interest to anyone so I refused to obey the spirit to report them. Besides, I felt the spirit was not a mature spirit because it continued to speak with the voice of a baby. I snuffed out the candles so that they would not start a fire and I went to bed.

In the morning I told my cousin about what had happened to him and about the voice and images. He immediately told me that I should become a Rosicrucian because I was able to withstand the spirit. I welcomed the idea and was excited about becoming a Rosicrucian but, as he told me later, when he presented the idea at their meeting, the leaders said that I was too young. However, I continued to read their magazines up until my graduation from high school. Some years ago, I met a former acquaintance from my high school days who had become an active Rosicrucian. I guess there was an expression of shock on my face at the announcement of being an active Rosicrucian and in response to it, this person said to me, "But you are the one that introduced me to the Rosicrucian Order." I asked the Lord to forgive me for this sin after I got saved because I used to give Rosicrucian magazines to this person. I continue to pray that this person will come to know Jesus as Lord.

Along with his Rosicrucian practice, my cousin Bennett also found a man who supposedly got some supernatural powers from India. I do not know if he actually went to India to receive this power or some other person gave it to him. He carried a heavy book that he called "the seven books of Moses" titled, *With God, All Things Are Possible*. With this book he would do divination consultation for my uncle's wife, my cousin, and my mother. One day I was around to observe his divination activities. I observed that although he used a bowl of water as a medium for seeing images, it was similar to the Rosicrucian mirror. I told him my observation, and of course he too thought that I should be in the same business with him. He wanted to train me but I discovered that his activities involved the use of actual human body parts and sometimes live human sacrifice. He claimed that on his last assignment concerning a land dispute, he had to bury a pregnant woman alive in order to guarantee victory for his client in the court case. He had no remorse about using live human or human body parts in his rituals. He told me that there is no human body part that he could not purchase. He wanted to give me the secret code so that I could go to one of the markets in Lagos and buy whatever human body parts he needed for him. I found the idea very repulsive but he thought I was naive. Not long after, his relationship with my cousin ended over a girl. He went away for good.

Also, during my last two semesters of my high school, a young lady started her own spiritism church in my mother's hometown where I was attending high school. It quickly became the teenage hangout spot in the evening during school break. The news was that this young lady was a virgin and could see visions. The music was the type that you could really dance to, so we teenagers loved it. She was the only one who wore the white garment during service. The other members were not required to wear the long white garment. One day some of my friends suggested that I go with them to this church and I went with them. I met the lady after service and she requested that I meet with her privately the next day before service. I went to see her and she immediately informed me that she knew that I was a virgin and that she also knew that I was called to do what she was doing. I told her about my desire to undergo water baptism by immersion. I told her that it was a desire that I could not shake off or let go. She told me the day to come back for water baptism. True to her word, she took me and some other people to the river and she baptized us. She told me that she only allowed girls who are virgins to come close to her and that her personal request to me was that she wanted me to start fixing (braiding or plaiting) her hair. I did her hair a couple of times but I was still not sure about the prophesying and visions that were part of her evening and Sunday services.

One day she held an all-night prayer and I went. Sometime during the night, she began to pace back and forth as she prophesied. She spoke in a different language (not the tongues of the Bible) whenever she was prophesying. As she prophesied, a teenager who suffered from epilepsy began to have a seizure and to foam in the mouth. He fell and was rolling on the floor uncontrollably. She went over to him and I watched, but she could not subdue the spirit. This went on for a long time and the congregation dispersed after a while. I did not go back to her church. I heard some years ago that she was now born again and was in a spirit-filled Bible College!

Before I left my mother's hometown in my last months of high school, my mother came to visit during one of the school breaks. She had been referred to a female witch doctor in a town close to her hometown. She was looking for a solution to one of my younger sisters' stubbornness. Since I was not the focus of this particular visit to the witch doctor, I decided to go along with them in order to enjoy the car ride. I regretted my going on this trip for years afterwards. While my mother and my uncle were inside with my sister to consult with the witch doctor, I stayed in the car with the driver and listened to music. Not long after they went in, they came out. The report was that this woman who claimed to have just returned from living under water for seven months with water spirits said that my sister and the rest of my mother's children were not the ones that my mother should focus on. She picked me out of all my mother's children as the one that my mother needed to be concerned about.

The non-Christian Ibos and non-Christian Anioma (formerly Bendel) Ibos in Nigeria believe in reincarnation. My mother is an Anioma Ibo from Agbor. They believe that in the children's world before birth, there are a group of children (Ogbanje) that love coming into the world to gain the affections of their parents and relatives. Just when everyone is so in love with them, they exit the world only to return again. According to this belief, these children actually love to torment their parents by dying and returning again to the world only to die again. Therefore, it was the duty of the parents to identify such children and to stop them on their endless journey between life and death. According to this woman witch doctor who had not even laid eyes on me yet, I was to be apprehended before graduation from high school. I promptly told my mother and her brother that the woman was wrong and that I was not an Ogbanje. They both challenged me to go and stand before the woman in order to settle the issue. All she did when I went inside to see her was reaffirm her words. I was so angry with myself for accompanying my mother on this journey. My immediate younger sister did not come along on this journey; she was not around to be picked on.

My mother truly believed the woman's report that something evil was going to happen to me before or upon my graduation from high school if something was not done. She went about sad for two days because I would not listen to the witch doctor's report. My mother, my grandmother, and my younger sister began to speak to me about the need to let the woman perform the ceremony to break the cycle of an endless journey in and out of life. We went back to the woman to inquire from her what needed to be done. She gave my mother a list of the things she needed to bring, but before she could perform the ceremony, my mother had to obtain my genuine consent. The ceremony cannot be performed against a person's will. She told my mother to give me whatever I asked for as a bargain for my willingness to undergo the ceremony. When she informed me, my sister and I thought about the possible things I could ask for. At first I chose a car but we decided against it because we knew she could not afford it. I settled for a party with my friends and a shopping spree.

Because the Ogbanje ceremony is popular among the Ibos, somehow the news got to my dad in the city where he was. He found out the date of the Ogbanje ceremony and he promptly showed up in my mother's hometown. Since we were no longer children, my sister and I decided to verify whether or not the Ibos' claim of removing an Ogbanje spirit from a person was true. I think in his own way, my dad wanted also to find out the truth about the claim. On the appointed day, we all went to the town to meet with this woman for the ceremony. She claimed that there was a woman spirit (a "mermaid") living in the river near her home and that this mermaid was the one that gave her power. Therefore, the ceremony would take place in the river.

Again, yours truly was dressed in a white cloth with a pot full of concoctions placed on my head as I was led in a procession to this river. It was the most shameful experience of my life. According to her, the spirit was in the head and had to be removed. I was made to lie down in the shallow part of the river while she made an incision on the left side of my face. Since the incision was close to my left eye, I was determined to see what the spirit looked like. I mean, I was not going to miss a thing. I watched as she in a very subtle way pulled out something that looked like a piece of gold wrapped with a black thread from the sand next to my head and began to show it to the people that stood by as the Ogbanje spirit that she pulled out of my head. I immediately told my mother, my sister, and my dad that it was not true and that I saw her take the piece of gold from the sand next to my head. She replied that I was making such statements because of my desire not to be rid of the spirit. But I knew what I saw. She conducted a funeral for the piece of gold.

When I obtained a visa to come to the United States, again my mother went for another consultation and was told this time that she needed do something else so that I did not come back from the United States in a casket. This time she had the ace. No ceremony, no U.S. for me! The woman who conducted this second ceremony could not circumcise me because I was already grown so she made an incision on my stomach. There was no procession in this ceremony.

I thank God that both my mother and my cousin Bennett are now born again. My mother is now one of the most active evangelists that I know and she is totally on fire for the Lord. Praise God!

In retrospect, I can see why the Lord took me out of Nigeria at a very early age in my life, because it seems as though I wore a tag or something that attracted spiritualists. Even in my first years in the United States I got a message from my grandmother that the idol god (Umomi) of my father's family was angry because his mother was not around to worship him. Her instruction was for me to come back home to Nigeria and serve the (dumb) idol in order for his anger against my family to be appeased. The proposal was not an option for me.

Chapter Three

❧

Events before My Salvation Experience

Upon receiving my master's degree from Atlanta University, I was recruited by the State of New York Department of Labor into the Management Internship Program administered by the Rockefeller Institute in Albany. Soon after my relocation to Albany, I realized that I had made a mistake by moving to Albany from Atlanta. Not only did I not know people there, I found the weather too cold. Being from Nigeria, in West Africa, I wanted a place with lots of sunshine and Albany, New York was not it. Therefore, I set a goal to complete the program and work at the Department of Labor for a few years and move back to Atlanta. My deadline was set for 1996 because I had to be back in Atlanta to complete my PhD program before 1998.

Waiting for 1996 to arrive proved to be one of the biggest challenges of my life. I wanted something to fill the years while I waited to move back to Atlanta. Meanwhile at my job, I had a colleague who had an overwhelming passion for the arts. He lived and breathed classical music. His love of classical music was such that although I knew nothing about that type of music, I was quite amazed to see a person so completely given to the passion and love of classical music. One day, he convinced me to go with him to Tanglewood in nearby Boston for my first experience of classical music. On my first visit, the violin immediately intrigued me. I had never heard a more sorrowful musical instrument in my life. In all the different musical pieces they played, all I heard was the cry of the violin. The violin fascinated me because it could cry out a most sorrowful, most beautiful, and most peaceful sound at the same time. Anyway, to make a long story short, I attended different orchestral musical performances with my colleague for almost a year. To my surprise, I had developed a serious passion for classical music.

At this time, I also began to be troubled by some dreams that I was having at night. Hanging out with my colleague and listening to soothing music was okay, but I needed answers to what was happening to me in dreams at night. As a result of the dreams, I became very interested in knowing the purpose of life and existence. I discovered that having a good job, eating good food, and listening to some of the best classical music made the vacuum in my life scream louder for attention and I could not ignore it. Against the vow that I had made not to get serious with anyone in the northern part of the U.S., I met someone that I liked. I thought maybe putting aside my analytical mind and getting married would somehow fill the void that I was feeling. While we were on what was supposed to have been a romantic vacation in California, an alarm went off in me and I could not shut it off. It was screaming, "you cannot marry this guy" and it would not stop. Still, we went ahead to try to figure out how to go about getting married. He decided to go back home and to inform his mother and my mother of our intentions. I did not know that his mother was a Christian. Her only counsel to him was that he could marry whomever he wanted to marry as long as she was a Christian. He called me from Nigeria to tell me what his mother had said and he also wanted to know if I would begin to go to church with him. Being a total heathen, I gave him an emphatic no and in anger I forbade him from going to see or speak to my mother. Because of the racism I encountered when I first came to the United States, my burning desire at this time in my life was to first know that God loves us black people, and then I would serve Him as He would want me to serve Him. Therefore, I refused to go to church to please a person. That ended the relationship and I was glad.

Soon after the relationship ended, I again began to receive a barrage of dreams about God and Jesus. During the course of my going to concerts with my colleague, I noticed a few things about him. He went to Mass faithfully during Lent and some mornings before going to work. He frequently went for a quick Mass at lunchtime also. He had noticed that I did not go to any church or practice any religion. Prior to this era in my life, and due to the secular education that I had received, I had become convinced that Karl Marx was right in his saying that "religion is the opium of the people." I was of a firm belief that if you wanted to mobilize the masses to support your cause, it was most effective when your cause was couched in some religious piety. I was rather disappointed when as part of my statistical analysis paper, which I wrote before the final paper for my master's degree, I conducted research to prove that people use religion to console themselves when they fail to achieve their goals in life. My premise was that the poor were more religious than the rich and that blacks were more religious

than whites because of economic reasons. My argument was that people believe in God when they come
to the realization that there is no hope of meeting
their needs on earth. Therefore they place their hope
in some afterlife as a means of consolation. But I was
shocked at the results of my research interviews. Most
of the Christians that I interviewed gave me answers I
was not expecting. I interviewed the rich, the poor,
and the in-between, both white and black. Most of
them talked with so much passion about their love
for God and their gratitude for His grace. When I presented the paper, I had to refute my own argument of
why people become religious. I remembered being so
angry at especially the black people that spoke to me
about their faith with so much passion. In my unre-
generate state, I just concluded that they had been
thoroughly brainwashed by their religious leaders as a
ploy to get their money.

Now let's go back to the events concerning my
colleague. At first, I did not ask him about his religious lifestyle nor did he make any comment about
mine for a while. Things changed when I had a night
vision and a dream that I considered serious. In this
night vision, the Lord Jesus showed up in my bedroom and said to me, *"You have a very studious spirit.
Your spirit has read the entire Bible three times and it has
counted how many references were made in the Bible to my
Father and to me. Your spirit is asking for an audience with
my Father because it thinks that there are more references
made to me than my Father. Your spirit thinks that I would
cause another rebellion [reference to what Satan did] and
that I would not deliver the Kingdom to my father as the scripture stated. Therefore, your spirit seeks to protect my Father
from me."* Then *without smiling He said,* **"I am the Way, the
Truth, and the Life. No one comes to the Father but by me,"**

and He pounded His right hand on His chest. This was the first time that I had ever seen the Lord Jesus without a smile. He was almost angry as He spoke. I got out of bed and I began looking for someone who could tell me how to have a talk with my spirit in order to keep it from getting me into trouble with the Lord Jesus. The last person I wanted to pick a fight with was the Lord Jesus. Therefore, I needed to know how to talk to my spirit before things got out of hand. As though the above night vision I just narrated was not serious enough, I had a profound dream.

*In this dream, I was with my younger sister (Josephine) who lived in London, England, but the scene in the dream quickly changed. It seemed as though I had died and therefore needed to go away beyond the land of the living. My sister decided to escort me on this journey and as we went, we came to a place that marked the division between the land of the living and the dead. My sister could not go with me beyond this point that seemed to separate the land of the living from the land of the dead. I had to make the rest of the journey on my own. I proceeded to go alone, leaving my sister behind. Not too long into the journey, a man dressed in a long white robe (I did not recognize Him as the Holy Spirit then) appeared with a broad smile on His face. He was so humble and so gentle that I stood amazed at Him. He noticed the fear on my face as He stopped to speak with me with a broad smile on His face. He told me not to be afraid, saying, **"This is where you come to receive your assignment and your assignment is to teach those children,"** and He pointed to a Roman Catholic Church building where some children seemed to have been locked up in an upstairs classroom. I could hear the noise of the children as He spoke and I wondered who had locked them up in the classroom. As gently and as quickly as He appeared, He left. As I continued on this journey, a figure clad in black from head to toe also appeared. He was* *laughing very loudly with his head thrown backward and clapping his hands as he laughed saying, "Look at you, look at you. I bet you are one of those people who believe that there is heaven and hell but I tell you that there is neither heaven nor hell." As he spoke, I somehow discerned that this figure was not to be trusted. He too also disappeared as quickly as he had appeared.* I woke up and was alarmed about the part of the dream that concerned the land of the dead. I needed to know if God was trying to tell me that my number was up.

Due to the concerns that I had concerning the night vision and this last dream, I spoke to my colleague about my dreams. He did not pretend to have the answers I was looking for, but he suggested I go to Mass with him. I went and was rather disappointed because I did not feel like anything had changed in the order of Mass or service since I had last attended Mass, and that was over fifteen years earlier. My colleague was faithful to his Mass so I went with him. I began to go to Mass with him at lunchtime.

One day he suggested we go to Mass in a shopping mall. I was surprised to hear that there was a church inside of a shopping mall. I was not prepared for the experience of that day. We arrived a little too early for Mass but there was confession going on. He told me that he was going in to say his confessions also. For some strange reason I found myself also going into the little cubicle after him to say confession. I remembered that when you say confession, you have to inform the priest of the last time you said confession. I told the priest that my last confession was over fifteen years ago and there was long silence. Finally he asked me what happened and why I had not been going to confession. The question stirred an intense anger in me and I began to blast the priest about the seemingly lack of love from God towards black people. I wanted him to tell me why other people of the world (other races) had mistreated black people over the years without God's divine intervention. I asked him to tell me how God could love us black people and yet allow some white people (missionaries) to come to Africa preaching the Gospel while at the same time other white people (colonialists) stole our resources and enslaved my people without His divine intervention. While I was going on with the questions of 'where was God' in intense anger, and ready to walk off, the priest asked me a question. He said to me, "Do you know Jesus?" I answered "yes." He asked me another question: "Do you know that Jesus is God's son?" and I said "yes." Then he said to me, "If the world will mistreat, abuse, and crucify God's own beloved son; why do you think that the world will treat you and your people any differently?" **For the first time in my life and during the session, I saw the cross of Jesus Christ.** When I heard those words, something in me broke and I could right there and then identify with the sufferings of Jesus. Neither the priest nor myself said anything else. I again remembered Jesus as my friend from the dream. I did not know that I had completely forgotten all about Him and had actually became angry with Him because of the history of slavery and the racism I experienced when I first came to America. I came out of the little cubicle trying to hide the tears in my eyes but I saw my colleague trying to hide the smile on his face as he watched me.

The experience did not make the dreams or my search for their meanings stop. I was so grateful to God for helping me to see Jesus in a whole new light that I wanted to do something to say thank you to

God. I asked my colleague how I could tell God thank you and he suggested buying a Mass card. In the Roman Catholic Church, buying a Mass card gets your name on the church roster in a given month so that Mass can be celebrated on your behalf on a given day. We went to the church and I paid the $10 and a Mass card was given to me with the date of the Mass. I have since come to know that God responds when your heart moves towards Him, no matter how small a move it is. That night I had another profound dream.

In this dream, we were about thirty or forty people caught up in a huge cloud in the sky. Although I had not read about rapture yet, the experience felt like a rapture experience. Because I love heights, I thought it was so awesome to be very high up in the sky in the midst of the clouds. While up there, there was a sudden change in the attitude of the group when someone in the group said, "Here comes God." I was surprised that fewer than one hundred people responded to God's invitation to come and meet with Him in the midst of the clouds. Despite the fact that we were few in number, everyone in the group erupted into a most powerful spontaneous worship as God the Father descended into our midst. He was riding on the wind and He had a branch of a fresh green "olive leaf pluck-off" in His mouth! I recognized the green olive leaf pluck-off in this dream because I had become aware of the Bible's account of how the Dove came back to Noah after the flood with an olive leaf pluck-off in its mouth (Genesis 7:11). He began to lay His right hand on the head of everyone and bless us as our loving father. From the moment He descended, He fixed His eyes on me although I was in the very back row. He looked at me with the broadest and warmest smile and with the olive leaf pluck-off still in His mouth. I looked at Him and I realized that I knew Him. His face was not the face of a stranger to me. It was as if I had known and seen Him before, and I was surprised at this. He kept looking at me with a smile. As others continued to worship, I realized that I did not know how to worship. I was about to start crying because I was standing before Almighty God and everyone around me knew how to pray, worship, and adore Him except me! I was disappointed at myself for not knowing what to do. Everyone was so caught up in the worship of God that it was not the time or place to ask someone to teach me how to pray or worship. He laid Himself flat above our heads like a flying Angel in order to be directly above our heads and to touch the head of every person present. As He looked at me, it was obvious that He was aware that I did not know how to pray or worship Him. He just smiled broadly at me as I continued to look at Him and Him at me. Then, suddenly, I remembered a song I had learned from church, "Our Father Who Art in Heaven, Hallowed Be Thy Name." I began to sing the song because it was the only worship song and prayer I could remember. Before I knew it, the person standing next to me and everyone else in the group joined me in singing the song. I was shocked to see me actually leading the group in singing the song! Still with a broad smile on His face, He said to me without speaking a word, "and you thought you did not know what to say." I was thankful to Him because I knew that He was the one who jogged my memory to help me remember the song.

I woke up and was very excited about the dream when a thought flew into my mind from nowhere. It said, "No man shall see God and live." What I thought was an awesome experience and dream was now another question of whether or not I was to set my house in order. I went into a state of panic. I needed answers and needed them fast. I began asking people about dreams.

I went to the Seven Day Adventist church for service. Although I did not know the subject matter of the sermon, I thought the preacher spoke intelligently and articulately. I decided to return the next time they had a service, but on my way out I saw where his Jaguar was parked in the pastor's parking space. I concluded that he was just another preacher after materialism and I decided not to go back.

Then I met a Jehovah's Witness lady who was more than glad to talk to me. I went with her to their Sunday service. On the way into the sanctuary, she informed me that they do not take or require offerings from their members. She showed me a little white box by the entrance door and said that whenever someone felt like giving something, they put the money in the little white box. Giving offering was not required! I thought, thank God that I had found a true church that loves God and that is not after money! Excitedly, I went with her again the following Sunday. She again invited me to their Wednesday communion service and I went with her. This is the day that I had chosen to tell her the real reason for my religious search. This was the day to tell her that I was looking for someone who could interpret my dreams. She told me that it was a communion service and she gave me a brief summary of the service that evening. She informed me that no one present in the church that evening was counted worthy to eat the communion bread or drink the wine. According to her, there were two people in this particular congregation that are now counted as part of the "hundred and forty-four thousand" people who will go to heaven. Therefore these two people were the only ones worthy to receive communion on this day. She proceeded to also inform me that both of these people were not in the service that evening. One was in the hospital and the other was bedridden at home. I thought, how interesting that the only two people who were worthy to take communion were both sick and could not attend the service. To me, something was not right with the picture. I watched them as no one took the communion bread or drank the wine. They passed the communion plate from one person to another and right before the plate got to me, she warned me not to take the bread or drink the wine. I was shocked at what I saw, so on the way home I asked her to explain to me why they would hold a communion service with the foreknowledge that they were all not worthy to eat or drink the elements. I wanted her to explain to me the purpose of holding the service at all. Just then, I caught a glimpse of God the Father smiling at me, as she could not answer me. I then told her that I was really only interested in finding someone who could interpret my dreams. She and her friend promptly informed me that God does not speak to people in dreams or visions anymore. They told me that my dreams were from the devil. I was so angry with them that I told them never to contact me again.

A few months after trying unsuccessfully to get someone who could interpret my dreams, I went home to Nigeria on a three-week vacation. I was recovering from an auto accident and I had also received a bad doctor's report. Most of my friends thought that I just needed a long vacation, so I took their advice and went home. When I got home, I discovered that both my mother and my youngest sister had become "born again." They tried to explain it to me but I was very skeptical about all the new churches that seem to spring up on every corner in both the United States and in Nigeria. I could not relate to the type of Christianity that they were practicing. They

did not use the Rosary in their prayers and they
prayed out loud!

On my first morning in Nigeria, my mother came
out from her bedroom and stood at the door to take
a good look at me after so many years. As she stood, I
saw a vision of "great peace" upon her and I heard,
"This is what you need." I heard the voice very clearly
but I could not understand how my mother, who lives
in Nigeria, where life is considered very tough, could
have such tremendous peace. She wanted me to go to
church with her the next Sunday. Out of respect for
her I went but I had my camera. While they listened to
the sermon, I looked for beautiful landscapes or people to photograph. I took pictures of a lot of the people in the church also. Nobody said anything to me
about going around taking pictures instead of listening to the sermon being preached. As for me, I was not
really interested in what the pastor (Chris
Oyakhilome) had to say because my mother had mis-
takenly informed me that she gave ten percent of all
her earnings to the church as tithes. She was trying to
tell me that God was blessing her because of her faithfulness to Him and because of her tithes. Therefore, I
was angry with the pastor because my summation
from my mother's testimony was that he had used
part of my mother's ten-percent tithes to pay for his
Mercedes Benz. I was waiting for an opportunity to
talk to him about it.

Four days before I was to return to the United
States, my mother insisted that I go say goodbye to
the pastor and thank him for his care of her when she
was sick. She made the appointment for me before
she informed me about it. When I made the excuse
that I did not know how to get to the church by
myself, she got one of my childhood friends (a

Muslim) to come over to her house to take me to the church! When she came, I told her what my mother was trying to do—get me to join her church and to leave the Catholic Church. I went with her rejoicing that at last I would get an opportunity to talk to the Pastor about the ten-percent tithe that he had been collecting from my mother.

I went to the meeting ready for battle. As the door to his office opened, I was ready as I stepped into his office while my friend waited outside. When I looked at him, I saw such an aura or a glow on this man with an unspoken announcement of "peace." It was the same peace that I had seen on my mother on my first morning in Nigeria. He stepped forward in the most humble manner and with an aura that totally disarmed me. I saw in this man the peace that seems to transcend any chaos. This was the peace I was told I needed. As I listened to him speak, it was obvious that he was genuinely interested in my well-being and that he had a wisdom that was beyond his age. For the first time in my life I found someone speaking great wisdom and I was actually listening! I could tell also that my mother had shared a great deal about me with him. Finally he asked, "Are you pleased with the way your life is going?" I shared with him my doctor's report and my search for the whole purpose of human existence on earth. He told me that I had done enough on my own strength and that it was about time I gave Jesus a chance. He told me to examine my life by looking at where I have been in life in order to see all that I had tried to accomplish on my own and the results of my efforts. He told me that if I liked the way my life was, then I should make no change, but if I desired the life and peace that God gives, then I should turn the steering wheel of my life over to Jesus, and he left the office and shut the door behind him. He returned about twenty minutes later and found me in tears. Before this day, some false prophet in Nigeria had predicted that the world was going to end the Friday of this particular week. This day was either Tuesday or Wednesday and I needed to do something before it was Friday. I did not want to be one of the people holding a one-way ticket to hell. So when he asked me, "Do you want to make Jesus the driver of your life?" I said "yes." Right there he led me to the Lord! At a later time, the Lord dealt with me about the underlying reason for my coming to Him—fear of hell. To Him, the fear of death and hell was unaccept-able reason for being in a relationship with Him. He told me that the fear of death and hell was what Job and I had in common. I needed to repent of it. He taught me that He allows anyone who has this type of fear to come face to face with the very thing (death) that they are afraid of in order to deliver them. This was exactly what He did concerning my fear of death. I repented and now I have a relationship with Him that is based on love. As soon as I invited Jesus into my life that day, I felt like one hundred pounds had been lifted off of me. When I came out of the office, I immediately wanted my Muslim friend to go in so she too could be saved, but she refused.

I received the Lord as my personal savior on October 28, 1992. When I got back to the United States, I was completely on fire for the Lord. I imme-diately went to a Christian bookstore and ordered twelve Bibles. I wanted to tell people about the Lord Jesus and I wanted them to have a Bible when I talked to them so that they could read it for themselves. I was extremely grateful because He saved me and granted my specified request to change the doctor's report.

When I got back and told my Jewish doctor about my salvation and healing, he did not believe me. He examined me and could not find anything wrong with me. He requested that I go for a second opinion. When the results came back he said to me, "If any more of my patients get born again, I will be out of business because I cannot compete with God!"

On my first Sunday back in the United States from Nigeria, I decided to attend the little church in the neighborhood where I lived. It was my second Sunday as a true Christian so I was up bright and early. I was probably the second or third person to show up for service but I was not prepared for what was to happen to me on this day. As people began to come inside the church for service, I noticed that they would go and sit in other pews away from me. Eventually the church was full and I noticed that people preferred to stand in the isle rather than sit on the same pew with me. I was the only black person in the congregation on this Sunday, so my initial reaction was to tell myself that I did not need them and walk out of the place, but because I am not one to give up or run from a fight, I decided to stay, but the exit lights were all the time very visible to me. The priest began the service and I thought, how hypocritical for these people to preach love and act the way they were acting toward me. A sudden resolve not to get angry or pay attention to what was happening came over me and I began to participate in the service. I was determined not to let anyone dampen my new enthusiasm for my Lord and Savior Jesus Christ. When the service got to the part where the congregation had to join the priest to recite the Creed, and as I opened my mouth to say the Creed also, tears began to flow down my cheeks. *Then, all of a sudden heaven opened and I began to see God the Father and the Lord Jesus sitting on the throne above the congregation. God the Father said to me, "It is me you came for isn't it?" and I said, "Yes," and He said, "Then, wipe away the tears from your eyes and look unto me alone."* I wiped my eyes and I again joined the service. This is how I received the gift of interaction with the Lord in conversations. Since this incident, and from that day, I could ask the Lord a question and He would give me an immediate answer! I went back the next Sunday and this time about three people sat very far away from me on the same pew. I decided to look for another church.

About three years after this incident, I was in Nigeria on vacation and I went with my mother to one of the local markets. After shopping, we were on our way out of the market when an unrestrained madman suddenly leaped at me in the market and punched my stomach and went and sat on a nearby bench as though he had not done anything wrong. Although he delivered the punch with a great force, I did not feel the impact on my stomach. Everyone around me who saw what happened including my mother stopped and waited for my reaction. When I looked at the man and he at me, it was obvious that he was not even aware of what he had done to me. I realized then that the devil wanted to do to me what he had done to the man (you will read about my encounters with this spirit in a later chapter of this book). Therefore, I looked up at the Lord and I asked Him to return the blow and to use it to dislodge those demons from the man because they disobeyed the Word of God that said, **"Touch not mine anointed,**

and do my prophets no harm" (Psalm 105:15). I blessed the man and I left. When I got onto the bus with my mother, the Lord spoke to me. He told me that he allowed the man to throw the punch at me because He needed to get His hand on the spirits of madness in order to judge them. Therefore when the man threw the punch, He (the Lord) grabbed the hand, absorbed the punch, and judged the spirits!

When you read about what happened to me within the first year of my salvation and my encounters with these spirits in the next section of this book, you will understand why the Lord needed to judge them three years later. He told me to forgive the man and to pray for him. Then He brought up the subject of how I was treated at the little church in Albany. He told me to forgive the congregation for the way they treated me. **According to Him, my soul came before Him and indicted everyone that was present at service that day and because of the indictment, not one single prayer has been answered in that church for three years! He said that He visited them (in me) and they rejected Him.** He told me that even the little baby who was baptized at the service that day was included in the indictment against the entire congregation. He wanted me to forgive even the little baby for the sin of its parents. He instructed me to bless the entire congregation and to pray that they would walk in love. I needed to release them so that God could forgive them. I learned from this incident that the Lord can judge an entire congregation for a single sin and that God can visit a church through even a new Christian! I also learned that I must be very careful about the way I treat people because God can use any person at any time.

I began to visit a spirit-filled church with my then-only Christian friend Adlene. I went with her to this church sometimes but most times I attended a bigger Roman Catholic church for service during the week. One Sunday I woke up and there was a spiritual announcement that it was a day of war. I had not heard of spiritual warfare so I did not know how to get dressed for war on this day, so I put on my new baggy shorts and top and stepped out ready for this war.

On getting to the church, I saw the signboard that the church's name was written on lying on the ground. It seemed to have fallen during the night from its post so I stopped to pick it up. When I stooped down to reach for it, I became spiritually aware that a spirit had actually thrown down the signboard and that the spirit was boasting evil things against the church. I said to myself, the evil it was boasting will not happen, and I went inside the church. Again, I was not prepared for what was about to happen to me on this day. I was not aware that the pastor of this church had cancer and that he was home sick on this Sunday. His wife stayed home with him. One of the ladies in the church began to conduct the service. She was talking about what I regarded as trivial things and I began thinking, can she not discern the devil's rage against this place? I thought to myself, the devil is boasting about the things he was going to do to the church and this woman is talking lunch and such. Ignoring church protocol, I went up to her in total disrespect of authority and told her that she needed to address the more serious things about the church. The ushers came and very nicely picked me up and threw me out of the church. I was angry and I tried to argue with the ushers when they threw me out but then one of the ushers quoted the scripture that says, *"The wisdom that is from above is first pure, then peaceable, gentle, and easy to be entreated"* (James 3:17). The Holy Spirit used those words to give me an absolute peace and calmness about what had happened. By God's grace, I went back inside and sat down till the end of the service. That evening, the pastor called me to apologize for the way I was treated but I told him that no apology was needed because I was out of line. I apologized for my actions that provoked the reaction from the ushers. When I hung up the telephone, I experienced what Paul meant in I Timothy 4:1, **"the Spirit speaketh expressly."** God the Father began speaking expressly saying, *"When you refused to let the devil run you out of my house after my church threw you out, I crowned you. When you made the decision to go back inside the church and you took your first step to go back into the sanctuary, I gave you the gift of wisdom; when you took your second step, I gave you the gift of courage; when you took your third step, I gave you the gift of power."* He went on and on and on about the different gifts He gave me this day. He counted every step that I took back into the sanctuary and for each step He gave me a gift. Finally He cried out, *"O daughter when you sat down, I poured my anointing upon you."* He then informed me that I had prayed for many different things that I wanted to see or that I wanted to happen in my life. But according to Him, my spirit came before Him and offered just one prayer that covered all that I will ever need in my life. He said, **"Your spirit request is, Keep me as the Apple of your eye, hide me under the shadow of your wings!"** He answered my spirit's request. After His explanation, I began to understand why *I usually myself in visions as a little child playing by the feet of God the Father as He sits on His throne reading a book. Every once in a while, He would look away from the book to* *watch me like any other loving father would watch His child play at His feet.* I also understood afterwards that although I had discerned what the devil was boasting against the church, I went about trying to help them the wrong way. I went back a few times but finally I just stayed with the bigger Roman Catholic church. The church was closed within a year afterwards.

What I did not know at the time was that I would need the gifts that the Lord gave me in order to overcome the **god-mother/sun-god** spirits that had already arrayed themselves against me. I was headed for major spiritual warfare and I did not know it. The Lord used the opportunity of my mistake at this last church to arm me with powerful gifts for the major confrontations I was about to have with evil spirits. I feel that it is appropriate at this point to give some historical accounts of the god-mother/god-father spirits. These historical accounts you are about to read are independent of the conversations I have had with the Lord on the subject of the god-mother/sun-god. They are the result of my research efforts as I tried to understand the god-mother/sun-god's spiritual strongholds. You will discover that the god-mother spirit is also referred to as the "queen of heaven." After the historical account, you will then read about the warfare that the devil unleashed against me using these spirits.

Chapter Four

❧

What Is a God-Mother?

So many people in Christendom observe the religious rite of becoming a "godmother" to children of their relatives, friends, and colleagues. They refer to themselves as godmothers and in turn call the children their godsons or goddaughters. They say this out of a sincere heart and a true desire to serve God and help nurture the next generation. So little do they know about this title "godmother" that they confess over themselves and over their "godchildren." Confessing to be a godmother means affirming the pagan deity established by Semiramis, the wife of Nimrod.

The concept of god-mother has its roots deep in paganism that goes back to the days of Nimrod and his wife Semiramis. Nimrod was the son of Cush, Cush was the son of Ham, and Ham was the son of Noah. He was the first person to rule the world and to establish human government in the "land of Nimrod" referred to in the Bible as Nineveh or Shinar. The Bible's record of him in Genesis 10:8–10 is this:

> And Cush begat Nimrod; he began to be a mighty one in the earth. He was a mighty hunter before the Lord: wherefore it is said, Even as Nimrod the mighty hunter before the Lord. And the BEGINNING OF HIS KINGDOM WAS BABEL.

Nimrod was the first man to form an organized society with himself and his wife as the sole rulers. The Dake's Bible (Authorized King James Version) gives the meaning of Nimrod as "rebel." The name Semiramis means "sea gift." The name Babylon comes from his city, Babel!

Legend has it that Nimrod brought home a strange woman (Semiramis) as his wife after one of his hunting expeditions. He then devised a plan to conceal her true identity. He explained to his subjects that she actually came out of the sea. He told them that she was an offspring of the sea-god (half-man and half-fish pagan sea-god) and man! Therefore, her name meant "a gift of the sea." This is how Nimrod began the legend of the female "half-woman and half-fish" known in the western world as the mermaid and in the Bible as Ashtoreth. Nimrod gave Semiramis the platform to control religious activities in his kingdom because of the story he built around her. Semiramis' true identity, according to tradition, is that she was actually a prostitute with whom Nimrod became fascinated and married. Queen Semiramis was in full control of the religious systems in Babylon. She plotted Nimrod's destruction when she became pregnant due to adultery and King Nimrod threatened to dethrone her, expose her adultery, and reveal her true identity/origin. It is stated that she had King Nimrod torn to pieces by her religious priests after she gave them her specially prepared "drink," and her bastard son Damu was made king. Semiramis then deified herself as the mother of the god Damu and she also became known as the " the queen of heaven." Thus, Semiramis originated the goddess system of pagan religions.

Another account is that after the death of Nimrod, queen Semiramis informed her subjects that her dead husband (Nimrod) had turned into the sun-god and commanded them to worship him as such. When she was later found to be pregnant through adultery, she claimed that her late husband the sun-god had supernaturally impregnated her and that her newborn son was Nimrod incarnate, and she named him Tammuz. She began to be worshipped as the mother of the gods. Thus the tradition began that barren women on Tammuz's birthday began to cut evergreen trees and tie ornaments to the branches. They would place gifts under the tree as an invitation for the sun-god to visit them so that they could conceive a child. Lights were set up in the homes so that the sun-god would not bypass the homes while making his rounds of visitations!

Christians ignorantly observe this tradition on December 25th of every year without knowing what they are actually saying and doing with their Christmas trees, Christmas lights, and Christmas gifts. This particular Babylonian tradition began by Semiramis is now celebrated worldwide just as the "queen of heaven" spirit desired! However, the Church of Jesus Christ will rise again in power over this spirit that desires to strip the church of her God-given power by luring her into Babylonian paganism. The Lord Jesus said:

"I will build my church and the gates of hell shall not prevail against it"

However, the church must be willing to follow the Lord in His fight against the darkness that seeks to swallow up His church. In his work, *The Rise and Fall of King Nimrod*, Dudley Cates writes:

Many different ideas from Babylon religion came down through the generations. Probably the key doctrine is that of the mother-son relationship. As the Babylonian people were scattered throughout the world, they took with them the idea that Semiramis had miraculously conceived and given birth to Nimrod reincarnated. Thus, all through the world, men began to worship a divine mother and godchild, long before the birth of Christ. The woman appears in different ways, and is called by different names, but she is always the same person: Isis in Egypt, Indrani in India, Cybella in Asia, Fortuna (the boy) in Rome, Ceres in Greece, Shing Moo in China, Hertha in Germany, and Sisa in Scandinavia but the woman was really Semiramis the queen of Babylon."

We can also see from the Bible that when Israel fell into apostasy, the people began to worship Ashteroth, who was known to the Jews as the "queen of heaven," as written in Jeremiah 44: 17-19:

But we will certainly do whatsoever thing goeth forth out of our own mouth, to burn incense unto the queen of heaven, and to pour out drink offering unto her, as we have done, we, and our fathers, our kings, and our princes, in the cities of Judah, and in the streets of Jerusalem: for then had we plenty of victuals, and were well, and saw no evil. Because since we left off to burn incense to the queen of heaven, and to pour out drink offerings unto her, we have wanted all things,

Semiramis and Tammuz

Indrani and child

Isis and Horus

Diana of Ephesus
and her 100 breasts

Devaki and Crishna

and have been consumed by the sword and by the famine. And when we burned incense to the queen of heaven, and poured out drink offerings unto her, did make her cakes to worship her, and pour out drink offerings unto her..."

Cates states that in his deified form, Nimrod the sun-god is known as Baal. Semiramis, as the female divinity, would be called Baalti. This word translated into English means "my lady." In Latin it would be translated "mea domina." This name becomes the name "Madonna," which is the name by which Mary is often referred to by the Roman Catholic Church.

Below is an illustration of the Roman Catholic "Madonna."

The Roman Catholic Church declared Mary the Mother of God after the Council of Ephesus (431). The Roman Church has represented Mary as the "Madonna"—the Virgin Mother with a child.

It is stated that the worship of the mother of gods was so profound in Asia, Persia, Syria, and Europe that when Caesar invaded Britain, he found the Druid priest worshipping the "mother of god."

From historical accounts and writings on antiquity, the worship of a "mother and child" or the godmother were introduced into Christianity by Roman pagans. **They were officially converted into**

Christendom and promoted and popularized by the Emperor Constantine and the Bishop at Rome around 336 AD. Therefore as true believers in Jesus Christ, it is our duty to find out what we affirm in our lives and exactly what it is that we worship. The devil is a serpent. He is very subtle. William F. Dankenbring in his article, The Surprising Origin of Christmas, wrote:

> Albert Einstein once said, "The Lord God is subtle, but He is not malicious." Satan the devil, on the other hand, is both subtle and malicious!"

God's plan is to reveal the mystery of his Word to believers by His Holy Spirit. God is love and He is so exceedingly wise that He concealed his plans for man from the devil and his demons. He teaches us believers His word and He reveals to us His plans for our lives. On the other hand, the devil's plan since the garden has been to get man out of the plan of God and to get man to worship him. He knows that Almighty God will judge any man who worships anything other than the Living God. We see this in the devil's proposal to the Lord Jesus Christ in Matthew 4: 8–10:

> Again, the devil taketh Him up into an exceeding high mountain, and shewed Him all the kingdoms of the world, and the glory of them; And saith unto Him, all these things will I give thee, if thou will fall down and worship me.

We must realize that the devil tricked Adam and Eve in the garden to yield their God-given dominion over

the earth to him. He immediately became their slave
master and they became his slaves. The Apostle Paul
referred to this in Romans 6:16 when he said, "**Know
ye not, that to whom ye yield yourselves servants
to obey, his servants ye are to whom ye obey;
whether of sin unto death or of obedience unto
righteousness.**" Once Adam and Eve sold themselves
into slavery to the devil, a very high price had to be
paid to get them and their descendents out. The Lord
Jesus came as the Lamb of God and paid the **ransom
price** to satisfy God's judgment that "**the soul that
sinneth, it shall die**" (Ezekiel 18:4). God the Father
was pleased with the price that the Lord Jesus paid
and now believers are out of the devil's enslavement.
**The devil's agenda has not changed. He is still
seeking worshipers**. He is subtle and very malicious.
He is out to get man to self-destruct by leading man
to worship anything other than the Living God. We
must not be ignorant of this for the Bible in
Ephesians 6:11 instructs us to:

> **Put on the whole Armour of God, that ye
> may be able to stand against the wiles of
> the devil.**

From the above Scripture, we see that it is our responsibility to know the Word of God and to apply it in
our daily lives in order to avoid the devil's subtle
tricks (wiles) of leading believers into idolatry. **Being
ignorant of the Word of God is a dangerous way
for a believer to live**. We must also not ignore world
history because there is truth in the saying that **those
who ignore history are bound to repeat it.**
Believers, who are ignorant of the Word of God as
Nimrod was, leave themselves wide open to the devil's

wiles. Nimrod's ignorance of God's ways (as narrated by the renowned historian Flavius Josephus in his *Jewish Antiquities*) led him to harbor a grudge against God concerning the flood that took place in the days of Noah. He wanted to institute a governmental system and build a tower so high that it would be impossible for God to carry out mass destruction again. Therefore, we who believe in the Lord Jesus Christ must know the Word of God and live according to the discernment given to us by His Holy Spirit as it is written about us in II Corinthians 2:11:

For we are not ignorant of his devices.

Also in Revelation 12:9, the Bible lets us know the extent of the devil's deception:

And the great dragon was cast out, that old serpent, called the Devil, and Satan, WHICH DECEIVETH THE WHOLE WORLD."

Satan's plan for the whole world since the day of Nimrod and after Nimrod is to get the whole world into one form of idolatry or another. He does not care by what means he accomplishes this. Believers' ignorance of the Word of God and the devil's wiles are particularly effective in helping the devil accomplish his plan.

In ancient writings, Nimrod is depicted as the one who taught rebellion against God. Nimrod was very angry with God for flooding the earth and for later scattering man all over the earth. He decided to set up a governmental system that he designed, to teach man to do things contrary to God's will. He wanted man to become independent of God. Therefore, Nimrod began the teaching of trusting in one's self and in one's own ability instead of trusting in the Living God. He taught his subjects that he (Nimrod) was the one who gave them their daily provisions and not God. He began to officially teach those under him not to worship the Living God but to worship him (Nimrod) instead. Thus Nimrod began the first state-organized rebellion against God.

Josephus has this to say about Nimrod in his Jewish Antiquities, Book 1, Chapter 4:2–3:

> Now it was Nimrod who excited them to such an affront and contempt of God. He was the grandson of Ham, the son of Noah, a bold man, and of great strength of hand. He persuaded them not to ascribe it to God, as if it was through his means they were happy, but to believe that it was their own courage, which procured that happiness. He also gradually changed the government into Tyranny, seeing no other way of turning men from the fear of God, but to bring them into a constant dependence on his power. He also said he would be revenged on God, if he should have a mind to drown the world again; for that he would build a tower too high for the waters to be able to reach; and that he would avenge himself on God for destroying their forefathers. Now the multitude were very ready to follow the determination of Nimrod, and to esteem it a piece of cowardice to submit to God; and they built a tower, neither sparing

any pains, nor being in any degree negligent about the work.

Chapter Five

❧

How I Overcame the God-Mother/Sun-God Spirits

I received the Lord on October 28, 1992 and beginning from that day, the Lord would visit me in visions and dreams to teach me scriptures. Whenever He saw me trying to understand a scripture on my own and begin to struggle for the meaning, He would come and explain it to me. I guess He remembered the last time I tried to read and understand the Bible on my own, and how through severe ignorance of God's ways, I turned against God instead. One day He said to me from heaven as I was trying to figure out a particular scripture; "Understandeth thou what thou readest?" and I said, "No." That night, He came in a vision and took me to His classroom and began to teach me. It became a normal thing for Him to come in a vision or dream and take me to the board in His classroom and to teach me. I thought then that every believer who got born again got taken to the Lord's classroom for a personalized teaching every week.

On May 18, 1993, God the Father walked into my bedroom and started speaking at about 1:00 a.m., right after I got back from using the bathroom and was getting back into my bed. Before He left, He told me to speak of the visitation and all that He said to me to no man until His appointed time. I was to seal up everything that He told me until the time that He released me to speak of them. When He walked into my bedroom, He introduced Himself by a name that I had not heard before. It was the same name that He used to introduce Himself to Moses by the burning bush in the book of Exodus. I was only seven months old in the Lord at the time so I did not recognize the name as one of God's names. When He left, I in my immaturity called up my then-only Christian friend Adlene and I asked her to guess who walked into my bedroom and spoke for six hours without taking a breath! I also wanted her to tell me if she was aware that God's name is what He said it was. Forgetting totally the instruction that I was given, I proceeded to tell her as much as I could remember of the visitation. As if that were not disobedient enough, I also told a few other people. At this stage of my Christian walk, I was totally ignorant of the consequences of disobedience.

It was two years later that the Lord informed me that although there were some generational sins in my family as well as other things that I, my grandmother, and my mother had done that caused the god-mother/sun-god spirits to target me, it was this act of disobedience that was the immediate sin that opened the door for the spirits to attack me. He told me to begin by forgiving Adam and Eve of their disobedience, which has made life miserable on earth, because I was no better than them. I too failed woefully just like they did. Just like them, I had no revelation of the importance of obedience. I believe that God allowed the events that I will narrate below to happen to me in order to teach me the importance of obedience as well as to use them as an opportunity to deliver me from the evil spirits that had already arrayed themselves against me.

I also found out that God has a shock treatment reserved for those who will not heed the gentle pleadings and warnings of the Holy Spirit. God can allow you to fall into situations or circumstances in order to give you an awakening about the spirit realm. He is able to save His children from the path of destruction even if He has to allow or use drastic measures to wake them up from a state of ignorance. As a result of having sat under college professors who were atheists/agnostics and an acquaintance who was a professed atheist, and also as the years went by, I began to think of myself as a "freethinker" without any religious inclinations by the time I came out of graduate school. One of the Lord's goals was to purge the "freethinker" mentality out of me. The events that I will narrate shortly will show you how He accomplished this goal.

The next Monday morning after God the Father walked into my bedroom, I went to work, and as soon as I stepped into the lobby at my workplace, one of the employees confronted me immediately. It was as though he had been standing there waiting for me. When I looked at his face, I was shocked at the image I saw. On his face was a deep black hole in the place where there was supposed to be a mouth. Spiritually, the man had no mouth, but a black hole that looked like a pit. He demanded to know if I now knew who my father (implying my heavenly father) was. Not wanting to be afraid of the man and his spiritual state, I said yes. Then he asked me, "What is His name?" Again, forgetting the instruction that I was given, I told him the name that God the Father had said to me. As I began to walk off, a strange "got ya" smile came over the pit on his face and I immediately remembered that I had been told not to tell anyone anything about the visitation. But my immediate concern was trying to determine how this guy who did not know anything about my personal life found out about the visitation. I spent most of that day wondering how he knew.

I was also ignorant about the power of the words that we believers speak into the spiritual atmosphere. The Lord revealed to me years later that when I shared the story about His visitation with my friends, I did not know that I had made a spiritual broadcast of something that the Father commanded me to seal up. The devils knew about my disobedience while I was totally ignorant of it and its consequences. Also, He revealed to me that if I had kept my mouth shut, I would have spared myself the following incidents that I am about to relate. But the Lord knew what I was going to do (disobey Him), but He loved me still and stayed with me through the ordeal. Not only that, He gave me the spiritual gifts that I would need as I encountered the evil spirits. Although He never left me, yet He was determined to make sure that I learned some hard lessons about the importance of obedience. He also wanted to purge me of the "freethinker" (agnostic) mindset that I had acquired through my years of sitting under atheist professors.

The Friday of the same week, I went to service at the church in the mall. This was the same church where the priest had asked me before I got born again (during confession) if I knew that Jesus was God's Son. I remembered that my colleague had explained to me that service was every forty-five minutes. From the day I got saved, my passion for the Lord took off like a rocket. I tried to go to Mass once a day and sometime twice a day! During my previous visit with my colleague to this place and other places for Mass, the Lord would caution me not to join in some of the practices in the church. They were things like taking the "holy water" at the door and applying it to the forehead, chest, and shoulders in a sign of the cross and bowing down to the graven image (statue of "Jesus") in the sanctuary as others did when they first walked into the sanctuary or when they were leaving the sanctuary. He also told me not to confess as others did during offertory that they were "not worthy" to have the Lord come under their roof. He taught me that He is my worthiness and that I do not need to have my own worthiness. He is sufficient for me. In obedience, I did not observe those practices.

There was also something that I saw every once in a while during Mass that I did not understand. During service, I would see a woman dressed in a floor-length blue dress with a girdle, and she had tiny stars around her head. There would also be a chain lowered from above with a cage and when it was withdrawn, it would carry what looked like lifeless bodies away from the sanctuary. As I look at the lifeless bodies, I would notice that they needed to be washed clean because their bodies and their clothes were so dirty. I had not heard of Semiramis and her self-proclaimed title of "queen of heaven," so I tried not to think about the images when I would see them.

On this day the Mass began as usual, but little did I know about how the Lord would use my encounter and the resulting events of this day to change my life forever. The priest stood at the pulpit as at other times and began the service. Not long after he began speaking, during offertory, there was a strange occurrence. It was not a vision and it was happening right before my eye. *I saw the devil enter into the body of the priest during offertory as the priest lifted up the cup of wine! He just entered into the body of the priest and took over the service. Instead of the priest, it was now the devil who was conducting the Mass! I was shocked at what I was observing. I looked around to see if anyone else was witnessing what was going on, but no one said or did anything. I quickly got over my shock and became furious because the church is God's house and the devil has no business coming into it. I lifted my eyes to heaven and called upon the Lord. I said to the Lord, "This is your house; what is the devil doing here?" Prior to this day I had no idea that the devil could enter into a church that belongs to Jesus. I did not know about open doors (i.e., avenues the devil uses to get into the life or midst of believers). I also did not know that believers could sometimes ignorantly give the devil access into their lives. I needed the Lord's help to understand what I was witnessing. Just then I noticed that the devil did not seem to care about the other people in the congregation but had zeroed in on me. He was furious and extremely angry and was pointing at me in anger. In my ignorance I thought, "What is his problem? He does not even know me." I too was angry with him because I was watching as all the prayers that the people were praying rose like vapor steams or smoke and went into the rustic silver bowl that the devil had lifted up. I cried to God because the devil was collecting the people's prayers into his bowl! As soon as I cried to God, the devil began to boast of the evil things that he was going to do to me. He tried to make me believe that I was going to be his "sacrifice" for that day. I wanted to tell him off but I did not know how. I refused to run away in fear so I stayed in defiance of his evil boastings. My main concern was to find out how it was possible for the devil to come into the midst of God's children during a church service. I could not understand it. Then as quickly as he had indwelled the officiating priest, he left. I was glad when I stopped seeing his ugly face and I was relieved to see the priest come back to his normal self. Not long after, the priest began to lead the congregation in the Lord's Prayer. Prior to this day and concerning the Lord's Prayer, I had a bad habit of substituting my words when it got to the place of "forgive us our trespasses as we forgive those who trespassed against us." Instead I would say, "Forgive us our trespasses as we would like others to forgive us our trespasses."*

As a result of having witnessed how the devil collected the people's prayers into his unclean bowl and because the devil had left, the Lord's Prayer was the only part of the service that I felt I could participate in. When the prayer got to the point where I usually substituted my words, and as soon as I opened my mouth to say my own words, the Lord pulled out a red-hot tong from his burning fire place in heaven and before I knew what hit me, He stamped a white cross right smack in the middle of my tongue! You could smell my flesh burning as my tongue began to sizzle while being branded by the Lord's tong. When He was done, I could not utter my own words as I usually did because my tongue felt dead. Immediately after he was done branding my tongue, the spirit of obscenity and blaspheming came and tried to jump on my tongue. It began speaking obscenity and blaspheming against God and it began trying to inspire me to speak obscenity and blaspheme against God. It could not stay on my tongue because my tongue was dead to every other word except the Word of God! I did not know how to fight him off but my tongue could not speak what he wanted me to speak. When the spirit could not get my tongue to move, he left. I immediately went on my knees and I thanked the Lord for protecting my tongue from ungodly words. I was alarmed because I used to only see visions and dreams but now things were happening right before my eyes in broad daylight.

At the end of the service, the priest placed the Eucharist in the center of a golden stand with a long-stemmed handle and a round top with sunrays—the *sunburst*. **The Roman Catholic Church calls it the "monstrance," but what I did not know was that in reality, it was the Egyptian symbol of the sun-god!**

Priest holding the monstrance used in the Church's rite of the Benediction of the Blessed Sacrament

I was ignorant of the meaning of the symbol and the significance of this particular religious rite that took place at the end of the service. All I knew was that at the end of the service, almost everyone in the sanctuary walked up to the priest and kissed the monstrance that had the Eucharist in its center. The priest had raised it up for the people to come and kiss before leaving the sanctuary. I clearly heard the Holy Spirit's instruction, "do not join them," as I stood in line. Again, in disobedience to the Holy Spirit, I thought to myself, the Eucharist is the body of Christ; why can't I go up and kiss it? My belief at the time was that the devil couldn't tamper with the Eucharist. So ignoring the Holy Spirit's words, I felt it was safe to go up and kiss the monstrance as a reverence of Jesus. So I went up to the priest and kissed it. **What I did not know at the time was that I had just kissed the sun-god symbol of Nimrod and Semiramis and that I had unleashed hordes of demons against me!**

What happened after I kissed that monstrance God has used to change my life forever. As I turned to walk away after kissing it, I began to see people as ghosts! I could see the spirits (good and bad) inside people as in an X ray. Almost every one of the evil spirits in the people I met tried to scare me like Dracula does in horror movies by suddenly leaping at me. Although they were trying to terrify me, I tried to be brave and not to show any sign of weakness. I left the sanctuary, and I decided to go into some of the shops in the mall to clear my eyes and my head by window-shopping.

In the first store I went into, the spirit of sorrow and sadness that was in the song that was playing on the radio suddenly became very active, and he too tried to jump on me, so I left. On my way home I decided to stop at the drugstore to get some over-the-counter medicine and a hot water bottle. There was a woman sitting on a bench in front of the store. The death spirit that was inside her flashed at me as I was entering into the store. I looked at the woman's eyes and I could not see the person but only the death spirit in her. I left the store and headed for my apartment.

Waiting at the bottom of the staircase in my apartment building was the woman whose apartment was opposite my apartment. She was twirling round and round in a dance while lifting up her skirt! She wanted me to watch her twirl and to tell her if she looked beautiful. I saw the spirit inside of her that was making her do the strange things, and I could

hear the announcement in the spirit realm, "Jezebel,"
but I had no idea what the word meant so I quickly
went into my apartment and shut the door. I went to
bed early thinking that whatever had happened, a
good night's sleep would be a perfect cure. I basically
stayed in my apartment that weekend. I did not want
to go out and encounter some more evil spirits. I
thought a good rest and minimal contact with people
was what I needed.

Monday morning I went to work only to see the
spirit that was in my next door neighbor as she was
twirling around two nights before, now active in one
of my bosses. I met her in the elevator, but unlike my
neighbor the spirit was now very feisty. The spirit
wanted to rush my mind and to seriously terrify me.
The woman said something to me but I did not want
to have a conversation with the spirit so I said good
morning to the woman and I refused to acknowledge
the spirit. I said nothing else until I got off on my
floor. Not quite ten minutes later she was at my desk.
She wanted to know how I felt and I said that I felt
fine. She commanded me to sit down so she could feel
my forehead to confirm that I was fine. Due to my
ignorance of spiritual authority and because I did not
know how to separate the person from the spirit, I
refused to obey her. The spirit in her gave a sly smile
that seemed to suggest the she knew something that
I did not and she left.

Later she returned to my desk and this time the
spirit had declared war against me. She insisted on
feeling my forehead and when I refused to let her
touch me, she called an ambulance.

At the emergency room, I watched in terror as the
spirit in her tried unsuccessfully to speed up my heart
so that it would beat too fast in her attempt to cause

my heart to collapse. This is the day that the Lord showed me that I would never suffer a heart attack for as long as I lived. I gained victory over the spirit that causes heart attacks on this day.

In the evening I was taken before a panel of twelve psychiatric doctors and nurses for evaluation in a closed room. I had never known fear as I did this day. I could see the little demons walking around inside some of the doctors! I was very terrified to be in a closed room with them. I did not know what to expect from them. At the end they left and shut the door behind them. From the awful sound of the heavy metal door, I felt as though I had been locked away in an asylum. I thought the devil had won because he had told me that evening that he was going to lock me up and throw away the key. I was left with two little pills in a little plastic cup and water. I was told to take the pills in order to go to sleep. I sat for hours that seemed like an eternity locked up in an empty room with nothing to do. This type of torture can truly make a person go mad.

When I woke up, it was Thursday and I was now in the part of the psychiatric ward called "E-ward" reserved for very mentally deranged and dangerous patients! The diagnosis, as my brother explained to me when I finally became conscious that Thursday (for they had called him from my job to come to Albany from Georgia) was "irrationally clinging to her Bible." He also explained to me that according to the doctors, for days, my one confession was **"God is love."** Because some of my close colleagues had also reported to my boss about some of my dreams and visions of Jesus, I was classified as highly delusional and bipolar. The doctor placed me on lithium and some other awful medications. When I challenged the doctor on the diagnosis, she asked me if I do truly see Jesus and I said yes. She said that as long as I was the only one seeing Jesus something was wrong. According to her, if Jesus were as real as I claimed, then everyone else should be able to see him. The doctor refused to discharge me as long as I was still reading the Bible. They told my brother that when I stopped reading the Bible, it would be a sign that I was on the way to recovery. My brother knew that I would not stop reading the Bible. Therefore, on one of his visits, he took away my Bible while I was asleep. He went through my apartment and collected the other eleven Bibles. He was furious to find out that I had altogether twelve Bibles. He called me and told me what he had done and why. We had a major blowout over the phone but I was discharged from the hospital a few days later.

After I came out of the hospital, I tried to explain to my brother what had happened with my boss and the spirit in her, but because he was a Catholic he did not believe me. He quite frankly told me that I had no business owning twelve Bibles, and did I not know that the Bible has been reported to turn people's heads, i.e., make them mad? He said that it is the reason the Catholic Church does not encourage its members to read the Bible. When he left Albany, he took all my Bibles with him. My brother was very grateful to this woman because he was convinced that the woman was after my best interests. She invited my brother and me to her house for dinner. My brother could not see any reason why we should not go. When I met her husband, whom they said had used his political influence to get me one of the best psychiatric doctors, he told me point-blank that God was too busy in heaven to visit me here on earth. He could not fathom why God would take time out of His busy schedule in heaven to come to my apartment on earth for a visit. When I asked him to explain to me the meaning of one of the things that God the Father did during the visit, he was confounded and he shut his mouth for good.

I thought my release from the hospital meant that everything was now going to be fine. About a week and some days after, I entered into another type of warfare with occult spirits. *On this night, it was as though all the occult spirits within the continental United States gathered together against me. I heard their voices as they declared that they had come to destroy me. They even had the fire marshal, policemen, and ambulance crews (spirits) as part of their group. Their goal was to bring me outside to where they were gathered. Although I was in a bedroom, I could see them through the window. Leading the hordes of this evil group was someone that I knew, and I could hear them instruct him to deliver me up to them. As they were giving the man the instruction on how to bring me outside to them, the room that I was in suddenly became completely engulfed in flames. I got up and sat on the bed as I watched even the walls of the building shooting out huge flames of fire! No entity could come into the room from any angle because of the flames, but the flames stopped short around the bed that I was sitting on. From where I sat, I could hear their frustration because neither they nor their weapons (firing darts) could get near me. Finally around 6 a.m., they all left.* I could not understand why they had all gathered together to try to kill me.

I returned to work some weeks later and on my first day at work, someone asked me how I felt about what happened to me, and I told the person that I felt fine and that the experience had actually brought me closer to Jesus. Not quite five minutes after I made the declaration, the same woman was at my desk again. As soon as she came, the Lord told me that her coming to my desk was the result of the bold declaration that my response to the question I was asked represented in the spirit realm. She called the ambulance again when I refused to answer her questions about how I felt. This time the Holy Spirit told me not to argue with her or reply to her accusations before the panel of psychiatric doctors. The words He gave me from a poster as I was being led to the ambulance the second time were, "God's love is gentle and warm." The Holy Spirit gave me the understanding that it meant that I was to stay calm and not to argue with them.

During this second examination by the second panel of doctors, the Holy Spirit told me to "remember the trial of Jesus and how He opened not His mouth to defend Himself," so I sat under a heavy anointing while I listened to the woman and the only friend I thought I had in the office report to the panel outright lies about me. They both claimed to have seen me chewing pencils. I sat amazed at their lies because only two days before the first incident, I had made a mental note to tell the office secretary to order some pencils for me because I had none! As I listened, the Lord told me that they were not the ones being examined. He told me that the devil wanted to use them to provoke a negative response from me. He reminded me that the panel was only interested in my reactions as they watched me. He told me plainly that the main purpose for this second panel of doctors was to test me for truthfulness. He told me that if I answered their questions truthfully, that He would defend me, but He would not protect me if I lied to the panel. Therefore, I answered their questions very calmly and truthfully.

One of the doctors asked me very bluntly, "You had a dream last night; tell us the dream." I could see the little demon walking around inside him as he demanded that I reveal the dream. I was very shocked and was about to become afraid of their spiritual discernment, but I had to compose myself in order to answer the question. Remembering the Lord's instruction, I told them the dream. I told them that it in summary, the dream was about how the Lord drove away hundreds of blackbirds sent to kill me. Here is the summary of the dream. *In this dream, just when they thought that they had succeeded in their mission, I cried with my last breath, "Jesus." As I drew my last breath, the Lord arose in me in full stature and all the evil birds fled away. I watched, as what had been my death became the resurrection of the Christ in me! When the Lord arose I could not see me anymore, but I heard the announcement in the spirit, "The measure of the stature of the fullness of Christ." Because I was ignorant of the scriptures in Galatians 2:20 that says,* **"I am crucified with Christ: nevertheless I live; yet not I, but Christ liveth in me: and the life which I now live in the flesh I live by the faith of the Son of God, who loved me, and gave himself for me,"** *all I wanted to know was, what had become of me? Where did I go? It was as though I ceased to exist and only Christ now lived in my place. Because of my ignorance of scriptures, this was of great concern to me.*

As soon as the Lord arose in my place, I watched as the Lord confronted the antichrist who personally gave the orders that I should be killed and I saw the brightness of the Lord's glory slay him. I saw in this dream what happens to believers at the point of death—how the Lord Jesus actually trades place with a believer right at the point of death! The very place where the believer's life stops is where the Lord's life begins. Therefore, no believer should be afraid of death because we have victory over death—the Lord Himself. I saw the man who had accepted the devil's evil "royal robe" of antichrist. I recognized the devil's evil royal robe because a few days prior, I was in a conversation with someone when all of a sudden, it seemed as though something split the person wide open right before my eyes and inside of this person was the devil's seat! I saw the devil wearing the evil royal robe as he (devil) sat on his stool inside this person, and he tried to make the stool look like a throne. The devil then offered me his evil crown to become his bride! He tried to make me believe that God would approve the union with him and he quoted the scripture, "The wolf and the lamb shall lie down together"(Isaiah 11:6) as his proof. I looked at him, his evil robe, and his evil crown and I said "NO" to his offer. He got very angry and he said to me, "You are a fool," and departed as quickly as he had appeared inside the man. Therefore, when I saw the man wearing the devil's own evil robe in this dream, I immediately recognized the evil robe. He (the antichrist) tried to act before the Lord as a great prince, but I watched as he was destroyed by the awesome brightness of the Lord's glory. The Lord later informed me that the devil is "not all-knowing." He said, "The demons knew where they were driven away from last night." According to Him, He drove them away from my body the previous night as I saw in the dream. It was the reason they knew about the dream. After I revealed the dream, the doctors unanimously wanted to know if I thought the dream meant my deliverance and I said yes. They then informed me that they had no further questions for me and that I was free to go. They told me that they had no reason or legal grounds to confine me to the hospital and that if I thought that I needed help, I could go ahead and give them permission to confine me to the hospital. I thanked them for their concern and I declined their request. When I left them, I began to wonder why the doctors would only be interested in my dream in what was an official medical examination. When I was confined to the psychiatric ward during my first encounter, I saw my boss shed tears. Knowing how hard the spirit in her fought to get me confined, I asked her why she was crying, and she turned to me with a smile and she said, "These are tears of joy." When I came outside, we met in the parking lot and I turned around and informed her that I was the one now shedding tears of joy, and I left.

I decided to request a medical leave so that I could go back home to Nigeria to find some answers to what was happening to me. When I met with my boss in a restaurant a few days before my six months' "leave of absence" (which she had to approve) for me to go to Nigeria, she informed me that she was an atheist! The Lord then directed me to stop being angry with her and to begin praying for the salvation of her soul. I had to learn to separate the spirit from the person. I must love the person but hate what the devil tried to do. It is the devil who is my enemy.

Chapter Six

∽

Attempts to Understand Why the Devil Attacked Me

The events that I have just narrated above left me totally confused but with an intense desire to understand why they happened. I could not understand how I ended up in the psychiatric hospital a few days after God the Father walked into my bedroom. I could not understand why the evil spirits were targeting me. I also could not understand why these things began to happen after I gave my life to Jesus. Whenever I asked the Lord why these things were happening to me, He would say to me, **"A city that is set on a hill cannot be hid and men do not light a candle to put it under a bushel."** Because I did not feel like a city set on a hill or a burning light at the time, I could not understand what He meant. But it was His constant reply every time I brought up the subject.

A part of me was happy for being born again but another part of me was angry because I was dealing with things I did not have to deal with before my salvation experience. The Lord knew how I felt so He gave me His word as it is written in Proverbs 18:1:

> **Through a desire, a man having separated himself, seeketh and intermeddleth with all wisdom.**

Somehow I knew what He meant by this Scripture. I was to get serious about seeking Him in order to find out why I was being attacked. I needed to separate myself unto the Lord and seek Him for answers. My request for a six-month medical leave of absence was approved, so I went back home to Nigeria. I had to go back to the beginning. Because I got saved when I visited Nigeria, I figured that I would meet with God again there and that He would give me the answers that I needed. He did not disappoint me. He made the necessary arrangements in Nigeria for my arrival. He had six radical believers (two of whom were attorneys) in my mother's house just waiting to teach me the Bible every day for the duration of my medical leave. My mother's pastor spoke a word to me that changed my life concerning the Bible. I told him that I came to Nigeria to look for God to explain to me why I was being attacked. He said to me, "Then be ready to look into the Bible because **God is His Word**." At the time, I did not know that the Bible was called the **Word of God**! I almost froze where I stood, and I remember thinking that God must have been laughing when I was packing up my Bible to go to Nigeria to look for Him when all I had to do was look into the Bible. I then realized that all the while I was looking for God, I had Him with me in His Word! I felt so foolish at the time. My mother's pastor assigned someone at the church (brother Tony) to teach me the Bible every week Monday through Friday for almost six months!

The intercessors in the church had been praying for me throughout the time I was in the hospital. They actually petitioned the Lord to bring me back to Nigeria for deliverance! They too were waiting for my arrival.

The morning after my arrival in Nigeria, I was standing at the doorway leading from my mother's bedroom into the living room, holding the open bottle of lithium pills and the other medications the doctor prescribed to me in my hand, when my mother, who had been watching me as I stood holding the pills, suddenly charged at me. She knocked all the medications out of my hand, saying, "I serve a Living God; therefore, my daughter shall not spend the rest of her life taking some medications." She snatched the gold cross I wore on my neck off and she told me to look to the real Jesus and not some golden cross! Following her clue, I went into the bedroom and brought out the bottles containing the rest of the medications. She took them all to the trash container and dumped them. She came back and prayed over me asking God to rebuke the spirits that had risen up against me. At that moment, I realized that I had to trust the Lord to deliver me in the absence of medications and a gold cross (that had been blessed by a Roman Catholic priest) on my neck. I felt a great peace about what she had done because I became aware that getting delivered from tormenting spirits was one of my main reasons for coming to Nigeria. I wanted God's hand to move in my life because I too hated medications. I did not want to be on those medications for the rest of my life. I thank God for my mother's boldness in the Lord because God responded to her bold move of faith. However, that night the occult spirits in Nigeria assembled themselves against me. Just like the evil spirits that rose up against me in the United States, I could hear their firing darts as they tried the entire night to kill me also. There was a particularly bold spirit among them (the spirit that

causes insomnia) that came close to the window of
the bedroom I was in, and she dragged her feet with
slippers on the concrete cement ground for hours in
her attempt to keep me up the entire night. In desper-
ation I cried to the Lord and He said to me, "Claim
Psalm 91." I picked up my Bible and I confessed
Psalm 91 over me and it cut that spirit off forever! It
was this night that I saw the instant effect of the
power of the Word of God. It was also this night that
the Lord first allowed me to experience how occult
spirits use ungodly thoughts as vehicles to enter a
person's life. As long as I kept my thoughts focused
on the Lord their weapons could not come near me,
but the minute I allowed my mind to wonder about
why these things were happening to me, they were
right there again. It was one of the longest nights of
my life.

About three weeks later, and during a healing
service conducted by my mother's pastor, the Lord
again came to my rescue. He opened heaven and *I saw
Him on the throne but there were so many voices rising from
the earth that were trying to drown out His voice and that
were also trying to keep me from rising up to meet Him. It
was in this vision that I discovered that material things
(objects like cars, houses, clothes, status, food, luxuries, etc.)
use thoughts as voices to bombard people's minds as they vie
for people's attention. Their strategy is to lure people to
hunger and thirst after them instead of the Lord. The Lord
spoke from heaven above all their evil voices and pointed to
me saying, "By my faith thou art healed." Because I was ignorant of the scriptures on faith, I began to wonder why He said
by His faith and not my own faith. He immediately noticed
the puzzling thought rising in me so like triple photographic
action shots, He rolled out for me the following Scriptures as
through a camera lens:*

"The just shall live by His faith." (Habakkuk 2:4)

"God hath dealt to every man the measure of faith." (Romans 12:3)

"The life which I now live in this flesh, I live by the faith of the Son of God, who loved me and gave Himself for me." (Galatians 2:20)

I then understood that I am actually living by the faith of Christ. Faith is a gift from God. From that moment, the fear of the devil, the fear of his unclean spirits, and their terror left me. The Lord informed me later that He would not shut my eyes as I had requested Him to do because of my fear of the evil spirits. He said:

The devil in his eagerness to scare you out of your mind, willingly exposed himself to you; therefore you will be able to discern him in areas and ways that others cannot discern him.

He also informed me that the devil has played a bad hand against himself in my life. First, when (through the Muslims) he willingly rejected my body for burial, and secondly, when in his eagerness to scare me, he willingly exposed himself to me. He said that I would no longer be afraid of the devil and his hordes of demons, but that I would be able to see them clearly in order to drive them out!

I still wanted to know why I was so viciously attacked. In response, *He gave me a night vision in which I saw myself as a little child trying to sit on God's own throne! He appeared from nowhere and picked me up right before I could sit on His throne.* When the vision ended, I was immediately aware that something was wrong because what I saw was the very type of sin that the devil committed. He tried to sit on a throne as God and was cast out of heaven. I was afraid of what I had seen but I did not know what to do about it. I was concerned about it because I knew that it is not a good thing for anyone other than God to try to sit on God's throne. One day when the Lord was ready to deal with the matter, He DEMANDED AUTHORITATIVELY TO KNOW FROM ME where I got the authority to sit as god and preside over blood sacrifice. He reminded me of the ceremony in which I was installed as "god-mother" to the idol god *Ogun* and the subsequent blood sacrifice I participated in. I immediately repented of the sin of trying to sit on His throne by sitting in the chair of "god-mother" to accept blood sacrifice for the idol god Ogun. I also repented for accepting the god-mother title O*gun* and I asked Him to forgive my entire family and me.

He gave me another vision in which *I saw the devil standing before the Lord as in a courtroom, contending seriously for my head. He was in his role as the accuser of the brethren and he was pointing furiously to the "Ogbanje mark" on the side of my face. Like a lawyer, he was before the Lord boldly asserting the right he had to my head because of the mark.* Immediately after the vision, I understood why my head has been the very place that the devil targets in my body to attack. The Lord also reminded me of my grandmother's instruction that every member of my father's family was to reverence my head beginning from the day that I was installed as god-mother. I repented for the sin of exalting my head against His knowledge. I confessed that He alone deserved to be reverenced and not my head. I know that He forgave me because He gave me another vision in which *I saw His name, "JESUS," written on my forehead with His own finger and in His own blood!* Spiritually, His blood has removed the "Ogbanje mark" on the side of my face. Now my head belongs to the Lord forever!

He also reminded me that after I got born again in Nigerian and I returned to work in the United States, I used the god-mother title "ogun" as my password on the login screen of my computer at work! He showed me a vision *of the login screen on the computer at my former job in Albany, New York. He wanted me to see how it looked in the spirit realm. Two years after I had left the job and moved to Atlanta, that computer was still running with the god-mother password on it!* Again, I repented and asked Him to forgive me and to log me off the computer. He did, because a few days after I prayed, He showed me another vision *of the same computer, and it had been logged off!*

I also repented for assisting both my grandparents in their divination activities and for the other ceremony with the incision in the stomach. I'd had no idea that the ceremonies that I had undergone were major sanctification and dedication to water spirits (i.e., mermaid spirit of Semiramis and Nimrod). The Lord showed me a vision *of the precious Holy Spirit. He found the white cloth that I wore on the day of the Ogbanje ceremony and I watched in this vision as He took it away from me and He carried it away.*

Also, He reminded me of the godmother covenant that I made with one of my elementary school teachers on the day that I received the Roman Catholic baptism. I had also stood as godmother to someone's daughter. I repented of the sin and I renounced the covenant that they represented.

The Lord also used my youngest sister (Pastor Bridget) to point me to the truth concerning the Roman Catholic Rosary. I used to wear one on my neck. I did not know that the Rosary was also associated with the worship of the "queen of heaven." I renounced the rosary and the Muslim beads and I asked the Lord to forgive me for having prayed with them. I repented of the sin of praying to Mary and through Mary to God instead of the Lord Jesus who is the only mediator between God and man.

With the Lord's gracious reminders of my idolatrous past, my spiritual eyes became open so that I could see how very wide the door of my life had been opened to Semiramis' god-mother/sun-god (religious) spirits. I then realized that when I joined the procession that day to kiss the "monstrance," I ignorantly presented myself to the devil to be attacked. The Lord gave me the understanding that when believers become godmothers or godfathers, they open a door in their lives to the devil and his evil spirits. The Bible talks about spiritual parents (e.g., Paul's reference to himself was as a spiritual father, not godfather) but nowhere does it refers to anyone as a godmother or godfather. There is a big difference between a spiritual mother/father and a godmother/godfather. The position or title of godmother is a Babylonian title that opens believers to demonic attacks. It is a position that exalts a person against the position that God alone occupies. God has no mother or father. It is the height of pride to think that a woman can be the mother of God Almighty. The Bible tells us in Ephesians 2:5-7 that the Lord Jesus,

Who, being in the form of God, thought it
not robbery to be equal with God: But made
Himself of no reputation, and **took upon
Him the form of a servant, and WAS
MADE IN THE LIKENESS OF MEN: AND
BEING FOUND IN FASHION AS A MAN,
HE HUMBLED HIMSELF...**

From the above scripture, we see that the Lord
chose to humble Himself in order to come into this
world as a man even though He has always existed in
eternity as God. **Mary did not give birth to a God
but a man.** This knowledge is vital because to understand God's redemptive plan through our Lord Jesus,
we must not forget that Adam lost the dominion God
gave him over the earth as a man. Therefore the Lord
Jesus, who has always existed as God, stripped
Himself of His God status and came into this world
as a one-hundred percent man in order to save man
and reclaim dominion over the earth as a man for
mankind (i.e., humanity). God gave dominion over
the earth to MAN and not to any other creature. Only
a **bona fide human being** (man) with a material
body can exercise God's dominion on earth. This is
why angels cannot directly exercise authority on
earth. The Lord Jesus was later indwelled by the Holy
Spirit at His baptism. After His resurrection, He
regained His position/status as one-hundred percent
God. Therefore, the Lord is now a one-hundred percent man and a one-hundred percent God! The concept of **god-mother is a heresy from the pit of hell
and it is inspired by the devil.** From the beginning
the devil has desired to exalt himself against God.
Since God has abased him, he now uses man to exalt
himself against God. One of the ways he does this is

through the concept of godmother, godfather, and the goddess system.

My attack was particularly severe because of the different levels in which I had ignorantly covenanted with the spirit through the different idolatrous dedication and sanctification ceremonies.

The Lord did not want me to let the devil have any glory concerning what happened to me, so at the conclusion of the whole matter concerning my attacks, He said, "I planted a seed (you) and I was just looking for the right soil for my seed." In other words, God allowed the attacks because He wanted to use them to develop and strengthen me spiritually so that I could begin to manifest the spiritual fruits He desired. He did not send the attacks but He allowed them for His own purpose in my life. Prophet Graham Cook from South Hampton, England stated it best when he said, **"God allows in His WISDOM what He can easily prevent by His POWER!"** Moreover the Lord said to me, "Your husband [the person I will marry] has asked to walk in GREAT POWER, so I had to send you to places that he could not go!"

The Lord wants us to seek to become spiritual mothers and fathers in His Kingdom and to help parent the next generation. He does not want us occupying the position of godmother and godfather.

True to His word, the Lord delivered me just as He declared in Matthew 16:18,

I will build my church; and the gates of hell shall not prevail against it.

This is the Rhema word He gave me to speak against the devil a few days after He delivered me from the devil's attacks, and He commanded me to speak and not to be afraid. **"Be not afraid, but speak, and hold not thy peace. For I am with thee, and no man shall set on thee to hurt thee: for I have much people in this city."** (Acts 18:9).

A few years after my deliverance, I received a piece of literature that had a picture of the **monstrance.** I was shocked when I discovered that the **monstrance** or **sunburst chalice** of the Roman Catholic Church that I had kissed at the church in the mall was **in reality the symbol of the sun-god of the Egyptian cult of Osiris, Isis, and Horus (the Egyptian version of Nimrod/Semiramis worship). I had ignorantly kissed the symbol of Nimrod and Semiramis in the church of Jesus Christ!**

Monstrance, or sunburst chalice

Over the years as I continued in my research, I have also discovered that when the Church was facing persecution in Rome and Judea, some of the early Christian leaders sought refuge in Egypt. While in Egypt, the Church adopted some of the Egyptian cultic practices in the order of their services. Also in Rome, Egyptian cultic practices were very prevalent in some of the Roman pagan religions. Therefore, when the Church in Rome began to compromise with the pagans, some of the Egyptian cult worship practices and the Roman pagan rites were allowed to mix freely with Christianity. This is why some of the Egyptian cult worship practices, Egyptian cult symbols, and the Roman pagan rites are still in the Roman Catholic Church order of Mass today.

Again, a few years ago, on the television station called the History Channel, I watched a program on the religions of Egypt. The documentary actually showed the Egyptian sun-god temple with a huge image of the *sunburst*—the very image on the Roman Catholic **"monstrance." It was the very symbol and emblem of the Egyptian sun-god and it has been used in the Egyptian cults thousands of years before Christianity!**

I must confess that I was very angry when I found out that the very place (the Roman Catholic Church) that was supposed to be a safe haven from the devil and his hordes of evil spirits has become the very place where the devil afflicts God's children at will. My anger is against an institution that has become an instrument of captivity of God's children instead of a tool of deliverance. Now I can see clearly why in the beginning of my search for the truth, the Holy Spirit appeared to me in a dream to instruct me that my "assignment is to teach those children." I love all my brethren in the Roman Catholic Church who are currently held captive in a Babylonian system of paganism under the guise of Christianity. My desire is that all those who read this book will seek to know the truth that was delivered to us by the Lord Jesus Christ Himself and by His disciples. We must be willing to separate ourselves from the paganism that is currently in the Church. We must be willing to return to the simplicity of the Gospel of Jesus Christ.

Many people who profess to be godmothers with godchildren might say that Nimrod and Semiramis lived thousands of years ago and that what they (the people) do today have nothing to do with them. They feel justified because being a godmother is done in the name of Jesus Christ and also in the Church of Jesus Christ! They do not realize that we who believe in the Lordship of Jesus Christ are actually enjoying the covenant that God made with Noah. Nimrod was Noah's great grandson and the Lord Jesus's lineage is through Noah. One cannot accept Noah and ignore the idolatry system that his great grandson established. Many people fail to realize that blessings and curses travel down the bloodline. I was one of these people. I actually used the excuse that Nimrod and Semiramis lived thousands of years ago to rebuke Pastor Theo (my youngest sister's husband) in 1994 when he tried to show me the pagan roots of some of the Christian practices such as Christmas. As a pastor, he taught his entire congregation to stay away from pagan practices that are in the Church of Jesus Christ today. Therefore, they do not celebrate Christmas. I really got upset with my cousin Helen, who is a member of Pastor Theo's church, because I felt that both she and Pastor Theo were trying to drag me back to ancient history by talking about Nimrod, who lived thousands of years ago. As far as I was concerned, their stories about Nimrod and Semiramis were ancient history to me and I wanted them to remain so. I told them that I had not even heard the name Semiramis prior to my conversation with them, so I did not believe that what they did long ago could affect me today. In their wisdom they left me alone because I was only about two years old in the Lord.

All of us who believe in the Lord Jesus Christ must acknowledge the truth that there is a need to cleanse the Church of Jesus Christ from the paganism that was brought into it by the Roman Church.

Chapter Seven

❧

The God-Mother, God-Child, and Christmas

Two years went by without me even giving a second thought to my conversation with Pastor Theo and my cousin Helen. In late November 1998, I was in my kitchen doing dishes when the Holy Spirit said to me, "Semiramis." I knew that I had only heard that name in the conversation with Pastor Theo and Helen. I thought about it for a while but I had no idea what the Lord wanted concerning it. I went on about my business. He kept saying the word "Semiramis" just about every other day for almost two months! Then it occurred to me one day to ask the Lord what he meant by the word "Semiramis." I then asked the Lord what He meant by the name. Immediately He said to me, **"A corrupt tree can never bring forth good fruit."** Again He said, **"A corrupt tree bringeth forth evil fruit."** I asked the Lord what He meant, and He told me to get out of pagan practices such as Christmas that had been brought into His Church. He told me that the real spiritual object that people worshipped ignorantly at Christmas was Semiramis (the god-mother) and Nimrod (the sun-god)! She was at the root of the pagan worship of "mother and child" or "god-mother." Then He asked me the following question: **"Did I not say that I will**

not share my glory with another?" I said yes, He did. Then He asked me what made me think that He would share a table with worshipers of Mithra (the Roman pagan sun-god)? He reminded me about the conversation I'd had with Pastor Theo and my cousin Helen. He told me that they were right and that Christmas is a feast of compromise between the Roman Christians and Roman pagans. He taught me that the very word Christmas is a compromise between Christ worshippers and Mithra worshippers who celebrate the "Mass."

In Rome, December 25 was regarded as the birthday of Mithra. In his attempt to unify Christians and pagans in Rome under his rule, the Emperor Constantine instituted Christmas as a compromised celebration of the birthday of Jesus as well as the birthday of the Roman sun-god on the same day. He wanted to make peace between Christians and Mithra worshippers. Hence the true name is "Christ-mass." Our God is not a God of compromise. The Lord Jesus did not say that he and some other god are the way, but rather He said, "I am the way, the truth, and the life." I remember saying to the Lord, "but Lord, the whole world celebrates Christmas," and in reply He said to me, **"Did I not say that that which is highly esteemed among men is an abomination in the sight of God?"** I replied that He did. Then He said, "I rest my case." I knew then that I had to take responsibility for that which the Lord said to me. It is now up to me to follow the Lord as He commanded me or stay in idolatry with its pagan feasts and practices.

I know that God confirms His word so the first thing that I did was to seek confirmation in the Bible. I went to my Bible and I looked up the words that He said to me in the Scriptures. It was most amazing when I saw it in Matthew 7:16-20:

> Ye shall know them by their fruits. Do men gather grapes of thorns, or figs of thistles? Even so every good tree bringeth forth good fruit; **but a corrupt tree bringeth forth evil fruit**. A good tree cannot bring forth evil fruit **neither can a corrupt tree bring forth good fruit**. Every tree that bringeth not forth good fruit is hewn down, and cast into the fire. Wherefore by their fruits ye shall know them.

Because Christmas has its roots in paganism, it can never be a good tree no matter how glamorous or dazzling its packages are. It is a corrupt tree and it will forever remain so. **Believers must not keep insulting our Lord and Savior by inviting Him every year on December 25 to come and share a table (Christmas) with Mithra.** This is what believers do every December 25th when they put up a Christmas tree and set up Christmas lights and exchange gifts. This is a Mithra worship tradition. Our God is not a God of compromise. The Bible tells us that our God is a jealous God. He is resolute and emphatic about not giving his glory to some dumb idols. Our God will never accept a table that is set up for Him and the sun-god no matter how many Christian songs people sing to make the feast a Christian event. He is not moved by "man's good intentions" to Christianize this pagan feast by tagging it as His Son's birthday while at the same time engaging in Mithra traditions of sun-god worship with the Christmas lights and exchanging of gifts. He is moved by the Truth—His Word. He told us about His nature in Exodus 20:5:

For I the Lord thy God am a jealous God.

And again in Exodus 34:14:

For thou shalt worship no other god: for the Lord, whose name is Jealous, is a jealous God.

Also in Isaiah 48:11, I saw the Scripture:

For mine own sake, even for mine own sake, will I do it: for how should my name be polluted? **And I will not give my glory unto another.**

In the Old Testament, we see in scripture after scripture how God delivered the children of Israel into the hand of their enemies whenever they fell into idolatry. We see an example of this in Judges 3:7-8:

And the children of Israel did evil in the sight of the Lord, and forgat the Lord their God, and served Baalim and the groves. Therefore the anger of the Lord was hot against Israel and He sold them into the hand of Chushan-rish-a-thaim king of Mesopotamia.

Also in 1 Corinthians 10:7 we see the Lord's admonition through Paul as follows:

Neither be ye idolaters, as were some of them; as it is written, "the people sat down to eat and drink, and rose up to play."

Because our God is a Jealous God, the Bible warns us also in I Corinthians 10:14:

Wherefore my dearly beloved, flee from idolatry.

One of the reasons that the Roman Church plunged Christianity into "the dark age" was because it embraced the pagan practices of Rome and began operating carnally in spiritualized religious traditions of men that had nothing to do with the Gospel of Jesus Christ. It was full of religious ceremonies that had no spiritual values. The apostasy of the Church was so profound that it was actually against Church law for lay Christians to read the Bible. Therefore the entire Christian world under the Roman Catholic Church was sold into idolatry and the traditions of men. The reformations since Martin Luther have brought the Church a long way from gross darkness to its present state, but we need to know what belongs to God and what belongs to the devil. Separating Christianity from idolatry practices will help the Church to move to the next level. The Church of Jesus Christ is called to a great height but we must obey what the Lord Jesus said in Matthew 22:21 in order to attain this height.

Render therefore unto Caesar the things which are Caesar's; and unto God the things that are God's.

We must be willing to do what the Bible commands us to do in II Corinthians 6:17:

Wherefore come out from among them and be ye separate, saith the Lord, and touch not the unclean thing: and I will receive you.

As I continued to search the scriptures, I saw in Luke 16:15 the words that God spoke to me concerning His perspective on Christmas celebration.

For that which is highly esteemed among men is abomination in the sight of God.

We believers must realize that God's ways are different from our ways and that He sees things from a different perspective than ours. He looks at the beginning and the end as well as the means by which the end was accomplished. Therefore, we must find out the mind of Christ in the seemingly innocent things that we do that are not commanded by Him. We must remember that no matter how festive and exciting Christmas may seem because it has been clothed with Christian religious intentions and songs, the truth remains that it is still a pagan feast and we must recognize it as such. Even if Christians do not wish to recognize the truth about Christmas, the devil does. He knows his own engineered and masterminded feast and he has been using it to financially cripple Christians and non-Christians every December.

On another occasion the Lord said to me, weeping as He spoke, **"My people in the month of December feast with devils at the devil's table. They then spend the rest of the year trying to cast out devils and they wonder why they are not effective."** He then taught me, saying, **"You cannot cast out any evil spirit to which you have extended an**

arm of fellowship." Therefore, it does not matter if the whole world thinks that Christmas (the god-mother, sun-god worship) is the most glorious thing that has happened to the human race. The Word of God to me is this: that if I, Mary, want to be effective in rooting out religious spirits and their works, I must come out of agreements with the spirits and stop extending an arm of fellowship to them. I must stop feasting with them at Christmas.

I usually skip church services in the month of December in order to stay clear of all Christmas activities and Christmas celebrations, but something strange happened at my church in November 2000. During one of the Friday night services, *I saw in a vision a very huge angel standing right in the center of the platform where the pulpit was normally set after praise and worship. As I continued to watch the angel who was standing at attention, my pastor rose from her seat and requested that the pulpit be brought to the ground level closer to the congregation. She made a comment concerning some Christmas event that was in the works. Because I do not pay attention to anything related to Christmas, I missed what she said. My concern was trying to understand why she had the pulpit moved to the ground level while an angel was standing right in the center of the platform to protect her. The Lord responded to the puzzling thoughts that were going through my mind by letting me see more of what was happening on the platform. I then saw that the devil was standing on the left side of the platform and that he had written the letter u on the ground. He was furious as he continued to underline the letter u in anger.*

The Lord opened my understanding to the fact that he (the devil) was addressing me through the letter u that he wrote on the ground and that his evil anger was directed at me. A holy anger rose up in me against him and I asked the

Lord what the devil was doing in a prophetic church and in the midst of spirit-filled believers? In reply, the Lord said to me, "But he [the devil] was invited!" I asked the Lord what he meant and He said to me that every time the name "Christmas" is mentioned or invoked, the devil automatically has a right to be in the place the name is mentioned because the table of Christmas was established for both Christians and pagans. He informed me that in His mercy, He sends His angels to protect His children when they unknowingly invite the devil into their midst. The Lord saw ahead of time that the name "Christmas" was about to be invoked, so He sent His angel to stand between the pastor and the devil in order to protect the pastor. This is the reason the vision began with the angel. The devil was angry with me because I was able to see him.

Since Nimrod and Semiramis sold the world into paganism, the devil has done his best to make pagan feasts and their celebrations highly glamorous and colorfully irresistible. It is true that a person will not miss going to heaven because they celebrated Semiramis's feast on December 25, but they surely will spend their time on earth fighting spirits that they could easily have reigned over. I grieve deeply as I watch some of God's children feast with devils in the month of December, and then begin to fight all kinds of sicknesses and diseases afterwards.

Over the years, the Lord has showed me how religious spirits fight people with poverty, insomnia, stress, anxiety, migraines, confusion, unrest, mental illness, lack, unemployment, vertigo, weariness, fatigue, fibroids, procrastination, sickness, diseases, homosexuality, and other sexual sins. They hate to see Christians get into the presence of God in worship or into the Word of God to study. They know that God's presence and God's word are the sources of the believer's power to defeat them. Therefore they seek to make people become preoccupied with how they are going to live from one day to another so that they have no time to serve God. They love it when Christians engage in religious forms that have no real spiritual value and power. They do not want Christians to have a meaningful walk with the Lord Jesus Christ. The unfortunate thing is that most believers open the door of their lives to these spirits in their Christmas and other pagan celebrations.

In my conversations with people over the years, I have discovered that with many people, Christmas is like a "sacred cow," and they do not really want to know the truth about what they celebrate on December 25 or whom it is that they really worship when they put up the Christmas tree and set up lights in their homes. Some actually get quite upset, as I did when I was first told the truth about Christmas. But there are those who hate idolatry and want to get out of it. They desire to walk in God's power. They want to do the greater works that the Lord said that we would do. Therefore, I feel that I should give a brief history on the origin of Christmas.

Chapter Eight

∾

The True Origin of Christmas

Any attempt to understand or study the god-mother and Christmas leads to the December 25th celebration of the birthday of the sun-god. The reason for this is because Christmas celebration is the culmination or the height of the god-mother/sun-god worship of ancient Rome. In Roman history, it was the period in which those who worshipped the Roman sun-god (Mithra) took the graven images of the mother-god and sun-god to the streets in a type of New Orleans Mardi Gras celebration. The practice began in Babylon when Semiramis introduced the human race to paganism and instituted herself as the god-mother, or the "queen of heaven."

The practice was brought to Rome in the form of Mithra worship along with the Roman Saturn worship (Saturnalia), which was in reality the worship of Nimrod reborn as the sun-god. As the "queen of heaven," the spirit that operated in Semiramis when she was alive desires worldwide attention. Therefore, she works through heads of government and heads of religious institutions in order to establish a national/universal worship system. Her goal is to have all nations, all peoples, and all tongues worship her as in the days of Semiramis. Nimrod and his wife,

Semiramis, were the first to govern the human race. They instituted human government and received worship as gods. That is why this spirit that calls herself "queen of heaven" knows very well how to entice nations and people into subtle idolatry.

The devil is quite content to receive this type of proxy worship through idolatry because it makes man "**abominable**" in the sight of God. Whenever man chooses to worship idols, God rejects the man and brings upon the man His righteous judgment because God is righteous. It is written in Isaiah 41:24, "**...abomination is he that chooseth thee [the idol].**" Again the Lord emphatically declared in Isaiah 42:8:

> **I am the Lord that is my name: and my glory will I not give to another, neither my praise to graven images.**

Chapter Nine

༄

Mithra Worship in Ancient Rome

Mithra is the sun-god (a pagan deity) who was widely worshipped in the Roman Empire in the early centuries. It was believed that he rode in the sky on a golden chariot and that he used the sun as his eye. Throughout Europe he was worshipped as Deus Sol Invictus Mithras. December 25 was regarded and celebrated as his birthday. The people of Rome embraced this pagan worship and converted it to their celebration. Therefore the Roman citizens celebrated the rebirth of the sun-god during the winter solstice period. This winter celebration was called Saturnalia. The celebrations began a week before December 25, and it was a period in which people gave gifts one to another, feasted, sang, and engaged in acts of lawlessness. The priest of the temple of Saturn carried boughs made as wreaths from evergreen trees and marched in a procession through the streets of Rome.

The Lord said the following words to me in late December 1998 as I walked into the sanctuary of the church and they were singing "Silent Night, Holy Night." He said, **"Is it not sad when the children of light and day come together in the month of December to worship and praise the night which**

is darkness? How then can they overcome darkness?" He told me to leave and go home. I went home and I have not gone to a Christmas celebration since!

Since 1998 when the Lord awakened me to the truth about Semiramis and her "god-mother" institution, I have discovered that just like I was, an average Christian cannot tell me why they put up a Christmas tree, decorate it, and put presents under the tree. They also cannot tell me why they put up the Christmas lights or exchange gifts at Christmas.

The idea of putting up the evergreen tree (originally fir tree in Rome), lights, and exchanging of gifts were associated with the Saturnalia of Rome, but their true roots date back to Semiramis and her story of how she was supernaturally impregnated by the sun-god and became god-mother. She claimed that the sun-god (Nimrod) caused an evergreen to spring up overnight from the stump of a dead tree, signifying the rebirth of Nimrod the sun-god as her son Tammuz. She began the practice of putting up an evergreen tree and lights for the visitation of the sun-god in order to cause barren women to become fertile and to cause the soil to become fertile. These practices were therefore part of Saturnalia/Mithra December 25th celebrations. Modern man has done nothing more than glamorizing the trees, lights, and gifts.

Chapter Ten

❧

The Role of Emperor Constantine in the Church

After he defeated Licinius in AD 323, Constantine became the sole Roman emperor. Church historian Eusebius, in his book *The History of the Church From Christ to Constantine*, wrote the following about Constantine's victory:

> His adversary thus finally thrown down, the mighty victor Constantine...with his son Crispus...won back their own eastern lands and reunited the Roman Empire into a single whole, bringing it all under their peaceful sway, in a wide circle embracing north and south alike from the east to the farthest west. (p. 413)

When Constantine converted to Christianity, he made it the official state religion of Rome in the fourth century AD. Prior to the reign of Constantine, the emperors of Rome were also the heads of all pagan religions in Rome. Historian Jack Finegan, in his book *Myth and Mystery*, writes concerning emperor worship as follows:

Julius Caesar was assassinated in March 44
BC; when an unpredicted comet appeared
afterward in July, this was believed to be his
soul taken to heaven. On 1 January 42, by vote
of the senate and people, he was declared a
god. Octavian, Caesar's adopted son, was
therefore the son of a deity and in 29 BC he
erected a temple for his deified adoptive
father while he himself was given the title of
Augustus (GREAT) by the senate in 27 BC...At
Athens a temple was dedicated to the Genius
of Augustus; at Ancyra (modern Ankara) in
Galatia there was a temple of Rome and
Augustus, and it still preserves a copy of the
long obituary inscription that Augustus com-
posed for himself, beginning, "The achieve-
ments of the DIVINE AUGUSTUS." (p.213)

Listen to how the Roman emperor Julius Caesar
describes himself in Josephus's Book 14, Chapter 10
of *Jewish Antiquities*:

Caius Julius Caesar, imperator and HIGH
PRIEST, and dictator the second time, to the
magistrates, senate, and people of
Sidon...greeting.

As heads of Roman religions, Roman emperors actually demanded and received worship as gods.
Josephus also says about Caius (the younger Caius,
not Julius), who reigned before Claudius Caesar, in
Book 2, Chapter 10:

Now Caius Caesar did so grossly abuse the
fortune he had arrived at, **as to take himself**

**to be a god, and so desire to be called
also...**Accordingly, he also sent Petronius
with an army to Jerusalem to place his
[Caesar's] statues in the temple and commanded him that in case the Jews would not
admit of them, he should slay those that
oppose it and carry all the rest of the nation
into captivity.

Also according to Josephus, Caius offered incense to
the statue of Augustus Caesar the evening he was
killed. Roman emperors demanded worship as gods
from their subjects, including Judea. King Herod the
Great of Judea gladly obliged them by erecting statues
of Caesar in the Jewish Temple while he was alive.
Therefore, Roman emperors could not tolerate the
Christians in Rome who refused to worship statues of
Roman Caesars. This is one of the reasons why the
early Christians were severely persecuted by Roman
emperors: because they refused to worship the
Roman emperors as gods or bow down to their statues. They were fed to lions, made objects of cruel
death in Roman sports arenas, and were tortured to
death because they would not worship the Roman
emperors. The church was essentially an underground church when Emperor Constantine came to
power. As head of all religions in Rome and upon his
conversion to Christianity, Constantine immediately
set out to unify all religions in Rome under
Christianity with the aid of the Bishop in Rome.
Finegan writes about Constantine's efforts to unify
the Christians and pagans as follows:

In the year 274 Aurelian declared the god—
now called Deus Sol Invictus—the official

deity of the Roman Empire; he built a splen-
did temple of the sun in Rome, and set the
sun's birthday celebration (nastalis solis
invicti) on December 25, the date then accepted for the winter solstice (also in his solar
character the birthday of Mithras). In the
time of Constantine the cult of Deus Sol
Invictus was still at its height, and the por-
trait of the sun-god was on the coins of
Constantine. With his defeat of Licinius in
AD 323 he became the uncontested ruler of
the empire (pp. 323–337) and was free to
openly accept Christianity, from which time
onward his numismatic representations and
inscriptions were only such as to be inoffen-
sive to non-Christians and Christians
alike...Likewise it must have been in this time
and with the intent to transform the significance of an **existing Sacred Date** that the
birthday of Jesus, which had been celebrated
in the East on January 6, was placed in Rome
on December 25, **the date of the birthday
celebration of Sol Invictus.** (pp.211–212)

Thus we can see from historical accounts precisely
how Emperor Constantine brought paganism into
the Church of Jesus Christ and instituted "Christ-
mass" as a sort of compromise feast between the
pagans and Christians in Rome. To emphasize this
point, Alexander Hislop writes in his book, *The Two
Babylons*:

Indeed, it is admitted by the most learned and
candid writers of all parties that the day of
our Lord's birth cannot be determined, and

that within the Christian Church no such festival as Christmas was ever heard of till the third century, and that not till the fourth century was far advanced did it gain much observance. How, then, did the Romish Church fix on December 25th as Christmas-day? Why, thus: Long before the fourth century, and long before the Christian era itself, a festival was celebrated among the heathen, at that precise time of the year, in honor of the birth of the son of the Babylonian queen of heaven; and it may fairly be presumed that, **in order to conciliate the heathen, and to swell the number of the nominal adherents to Christianity**, the same festival was adopted by the Roman Church, giving it the name of Christ. This **tendency on the part of Christians to meet paganism half-way** was very early developed...That Christmas was originally a pagan festival is beyond all doubt. The time of the year, and the ceremonies with which it is still celebrated, prove its origin. In Egypt, the son of Isis, the Egyptian title for the queen of heaven, was born at this very time, "about the time of the winter solstice." The very name by which Christmas is popularly known...Yule-day—proves at once its pagan and Babylonian origin. "Yule" is the Chaldee name for an "infant" or "little child;" and as the 25th of December was called by...pagan Anglo-Saxon ancestors, "Yule-day" or the "Child's day," and the night that proceeded it, "Mother-night," long before they came in contact with Christianity, that sufficiently proves its real character. (p. 92-93)

We who want to live by the Word of God and wish to forsake paganism must be willing to recognize the compromise between Christians and pagans instituted by Constantine, and we must be willing to stand for righteousness in order to become effective in carrying out the Lord's great commission. Dankenbring vehemently denounced the compromise with paganism this way:

> That's what happened! Apostatizing Christianity jumped in bed with paganism! The wicked apostate Church fornicated spiritually with the heathen, pagan religions of the world, and "ADOPTED" the date of December 25th as the "birth-day" of Jesus Christ, who was born nowhere NEAR that time of the year! This date was however, the birthday of MITHRA, and SOL INVICTUS, "THE UNCONQUERABLE SUN—THE PAGAN SUN-GOD!

He stressed the fact that:

> It should be absolutely clear that Christmas is a pagan celebration, pagan to the core, and in every respect has pagan connotation, significance, and hidden meanings.

Looking at the historical accounts on the origin of Christmas, it is clear to see why some historians declare that **instead of destroying paganism, the Roman Catholic Church adopted it**. Because the Roman Catholic Church rose up to fill the vacuum that was created by the fall of the Roman Empire, it became the ruling authority. The Bishop in Rome (now Pope) and the other bishops elevated their positions to stately positions and became only interested in maintaining their prestigious positions of power. While they were fascinated by acquisition of power and wealth, pagan practices and the doctrines of men were freely mixed with Christian doctrines. As a result, Christianity was plunged into the "dark age."

The question we must now ask ourselves concerning Christmas (sun-god, god-mother worship) is: What type of a Christian do I want to be? Do I want to obey the Word of God to **"Flee from idolatry?"** Do I want an effective Christian walk or do I want to follow the status quo? I have discovered that those whose hearts are truly after serving God according to His word do not want to remain in idolatry. Therefore, this book is really dedicated to these people and I hope that it will **help them to separate the chaff from the wheat** so that they can be effective in pulling down the religious spirits that now oppress them.

Conclusion

A lot of Christians think that paganism and idolatry are found only in Africa and some of the other less developed countries of the world. The truth is that paganism and idolatry are all over the world and in the Church today. The difference is that in Western countries, they are highly glamorized and they appear very colorful and festive. The world system of big business has tapped into the gold mine that the pagan festivities like Christmas have come to represent. A close examination of the fruits of these festivities will reveal the nature of the tree. The Lord is right; **"A corrupt tree cannot bring forth good fruit."**

The Word of God tells us in Proverbs 4:7 that:

Wisdom is the principal thing; therefore get wisdom: with all thy getting, get understanding.

Seeing that we are in the last days, we must examine our lives and know the truth about some of our Christian practices, because these are not the days to live in ignorance. Those who are ignorant of the Word of God and the wiles of the devil leave themselves open to be attacked by the devil in these last days. My experience concerning the attacks I suffered as a result of my ignorance of the Word of God and the truth about pagan practices in the Church bears witness to this. Therefore, I feel that if this book helps even just one person to overcome ignorance and to avoid the attacks of the devil, then my efforts in writing this book will not be a waste of time.

I am trusting the Lord that many who read this book will desire to examine closely the traditions that have no biblical basis whatsoever, which have been passed onto them by their parents and their grandparents. I further trust the Lord to help them become willing to come out of idolatry and to take a stand for righteousness.

There is an African saying that "a word is enough for the wise." Also, the Lord Jesus said in Revelation 2:7, **"He hath an ear, let him hear what the Spirit saith unto the churches."** God does not force anyone to do or not do anything. It is the domain of the devil to force or coerce people to do or not do things. As the good Shepherd, the Lord wants us to hear his voice and to obey His voice (His word). Therefore, I trust that the Lord Holy Spirit will help every single person who reads this book to examine his or her heart closely concerning the so-called Christian practices such as godmother, godfather, Christmas, etc. so that they can clearly see their pagan roots and their pagan fruits.

Bibliography

Cates, Dudley F. *The Rise and Fall of King Nimrod.* Raleigh, NC: Ivy House Publishing Group, 1999.

Chick, Jack T. *Are Roman Catholics Christians?* Chick Publications, 1985.

Dake, Jennings F. *Dake's Annotated Reference Bible.* Lawrenceville, GA: Dake Bible Sales, Inc., 1961.

Dankenbring, William F. The Surprising Origin of Christmas. Thousand Oaks, CA: Triumph Prophetic Ministries.

Eusebius. *History of The Church From Christ To Constantine.* Barnes & Nobles, by arrangement with Penguin Books, Inc., 1995.

Finegan, Jack. *Myth and Mystery: An Introduction to the Pagan Religions of the Biblical World.* Grand Rapids, MI: Baker Books, 1989.

Hislop, Alexander. *The Two Babylons.* Ontario: Chick Publications.

William Whiston, trans. *The New Complete Works of Josephus.* Grand Rapids, MI: Kregel Publications, 1999.

Printed in the United States
73718LV00001B/253-258